FLORIDA'S INVADERS

How Introduced Invasive and Non-Native Species are Changing the Ecology and Environment of the Sunshine State

by Lenny Flank

Red and Black Publishers, Florida

Contents

Introduction

Like Florida's human population, which has grown steadily as outsiders move in from the North and West, the Sunshine State's animal and plant populations have also grown, as non-native outsiders have moved in.

An "invader" species, simply put, is any non-native plant or animal that has become established from the outside. Some invaders, such as the familiar Honeybee (originally native to Europe) or the wild carrot Queen Anne's Lace (native to northern Africa), have settled harmlessly into the existing Florida ecosystem and have even become beneficial parts of it. But many other invaders have become serious dangers.

In the wild, most species have evolved together for millions of years, and have formed a complex and interlocking web of ecological relationships. Predator populations are naturally limited by the number of prey animals that are available to them, and prey animal populations are in turn limited by the amount of food, shelters, and other ecological requirements that they can find. When one part of the ecosystem begins to fall out of balance—if unusual weather produces a bumper crop of food plants, for instance, the other elements will naturally adjust to compensate; more herbivores will appear to eat the plants, and as the plants decline through grazing and browsing, the herbivore population will fall as the food source returns to its normal level. In this way, ecosystems maintain a "balance of nature" in which every part helps to keep the others in check and thereby maintains the ecosystem as a whole.

In most cases, exotic species which come from outside the local ecosystem, either accidentally or by deliberate introduction, are unable to compete with the already-established natives, and they either die off or eke out an inconspicuous bare existence. A very small number of introduced species will, however, find themselves by chance well-suited to the new ecosystem, and be able to not only win a place in it, but to upset the entire delicate system of checks and balances. In an environment where they lack their native predators and therefore have no natural controls on their population, "invasive" species can explode and throw the entire ecosystem out of balance, by monopolizing all the food sources, for instance, or occupying all the suitable habitats or nesting sites. The native species have no evolutionary experience of the new invaders, and no way to fight back. As a result, the natives decline and die out. What was once a thriving diverse ecosystem can be reduced to a monoculture as the invasive plant or animal completely dominates everything.

Some examples of the global devastation that have resulted from invasive species are well-known. The accidental introduction of the Brown Tree Snake into the islands of the Pacific Ocean has driven many species of birds, who have no experience of snakes and no natural defenses against them, to extinction. The deliberate introduction of Cane Toads into Australia (as a way of controlling agricultural insect pests) backfired when the giant toads took over the countryside, ate most of the smaller wildlife, and poisoned much of the larger predators. Goats that have been transported to islands all over the world have gone feral and eaten all the available food plants, turning the area into a denuded scrubland and destroying the habitat.

Even ordinary pets have become a danger: introduced into islands, domestic and escaped/feral housecats have wiped out all of the birds and small mammals, and in the continental US housecats kill an estimated 450 million birds per year. Other more exotic pets, ranging from birds to fish, have been introduced into non-native areas when people who no longer want them release them into the local wild. It has destroyed entire ecosystems.

In the US, we already have around 4,000 species of non-native plants, and 2,000 exotic animals. There are over 200 species of non-native mammals in the US, and over 50 species of non-native snake, turtle or lizard. About ten percent of all the bird species currently in the US are non-native.

Not all non-native "invaders" are "invasive", though. Many of Florida's introduced species have been pretty benign, doing little damage and posing almost no threat to native plants or animals. Indeed, some of Florida's invaders got here all on their own without any human help, through natural expansion of their normal range. But it is mostly the human-introduced invasives who get all the attention.

And in fact the effect of this invasion has been devastating. Already, some 40% of all threatened and endangered species are primarily caused by the presence of exotic invasives. "Invasive species" are the second-leading cause of species extinction in the world; only "habitat loss" kills off more species. It has been estimated that the presence of invading alien species costs the US over $120 billion per year in agricultural losses and in the costs of efforts to control or eliminate the invaders.

Because of its subtropical habitat, its diversity of ecosystems (ranging from tropical reefs to dry upland scrub forests), and its position as a center for the import of plants and animals from overseas, Florida has been particularly vulnerable to invasive species. Over 500 different non-native species have been found in the state, everything from Burmese Pythons to Kudzu plants, and officials spend over $300 million a year on attempts to control or eradicate them.

Florida's invaders have taken many different pathways to get here. Some, like the Love Bugs, spread here naturally from similar ecosystems that are nearby, crossing over land or ocean to reach our shores. Some, like the Green Mussel, stowed away aboard a ship and were unintentionally carried here. And a few, like the Tilapia, were originally brought here to be commercially raised as food animals, and escaped into the wild.

But by far the biggest factor in the introduction of non-native species to Florida has been the pet trade. The exotic pet industry is huge: each year, people in the US spend about $15 billion on the purchase of wild pets, ranging from Bengal tigers to aquarium fish. The majority of these animals are taken from the wild and imported into the US. A smaller percentage are captive-bred in commercial breeding centers.

The importers, breeders, and the pet-keeper are all pathways for the introduction of invader and invasive species. Because Florida has a tropical climate, it is well-suited for commercial breeders who want to produce animals like parrots, snakes, turtles, or aquarium fish for the pet market, or exotic plants for the garden and landscaping market. And from the 1950's, the ports of Miami and Tampa Bay have been the primary entry points for live exotic plants and animals shipped from

South America and Africa. Inevitably, there have been accidental escapes, and when enough individuals have entered the wild areas around these cities, they are often able to establish a breeding population. During Florida's periodic hurricanes, entire breeding or animal-storage facilities may be damaged or destroyed, leading to mass escapes.

But the most common (and preventable) sources of introduction are exotic pet owners who find themselves either unwilling or unable to care for their animal. Thinking they are doing their pet a favor, they often release it into some wild area. Most of the time, this is a death sentence; the exotic animal will be unable to adapt to the unfamiliar environment, and will either die from starvation or be snapped up and eaten by some predator. But sometimes a particular species may be able to not only survive, but thrive—and a new invasive species appears. Among the plants and animals from the exotic pet trade that have now become established in Florida are the Burmese Python, the Water Hyacinth, the Green Iguana, the Hydrilla, and the Lionfish.

To combat the problem, Florida has imposed a set of legal regulations concerning exotic species. Many species are now listed as "conditional": they cannot be kept without a permit, and the permit lists a number of requirements for secure housing and containment to prevent escapes. Other species are "prohibited": they can only be kept by research centers or zoos with proper facilities. But for much of Florida, sadly, this is a case of "too little, too late". No matter where you go in Florida today, you are very likely to see a number of plants and animals that are not supposed to be here.

Can Florida's Invaders be defeated? It does not seem hopeful. There are so many species here now, with so many of them being well-established, that it seems unlikely we will ever be able to remove them all. At best, we can work to minimize the damage they cause, to try to keep them at a controllable level, and to do what we can to prevent any new invaders from arriving.

The Burmese Python

By far, the most famous and best-known of all Florida's invasives is the Burmese Python.

The Burmese Python (*Python bivittatus*) is a large constrictor snake found in the rainforests of southeast Asia, usually near water. Some authorities consider it a geographical subspecies of the very similar Indian Python (*Python molurus*). At measured lengths near 20 feet, it is the third-largest snake in the world—only the Reticulated Python and the Green Anaconda are bigger. The largest known Burmese Python was a resident of the Serpent Safari reptile park in Illinois—"Baby" measured 18 feet 10 inches long and was, sadly, grossly obese, weighing 403 pounds. A typical Burmese Python adult will measure around 14 feet and weigh around 90 pounds (the females are larger than the males). Males can be recognized by the pair of clawlike breeding spurs located on either side of their vent—all that remains of their hind legs.

Like all pythons, Burmese are egg-layers. The females lay clutches of 20-30 oblong eggs, with soft leathery shells. Unlike most snakes, however, which simply lay their eggs and forget them, the pythons provide maternal care—the female curls her body around the clutch and uses muscular contractions to raise her body temperature above that of the surrounding air, incubating the eggs. The youngsters are about two feet long when they emerge, ready to wander off and live on their own. Under good conditions, they can reach eight feet in length by their first birthday, and reach their adult size of 12-14 feet in 2-3 years. Like all reptiles, they keep growing for most of their life, though their growth rate gets slower and slower with age. Burmese Pythons can live 25-30 years.

Pythons are ambush predators, lying in wait along watercourses and jungle paths for prey to wander within reach. They have no venom, but kill their prey through constriction, seizing the prey with their recurved teeth and wrapping their body coils around it. Contrary to popular belief, they do not crush their prey to death and do not break any bones; instead, they exert a steady pressure that prevents the prey's chest cavity from expanding, preventing it from inhaling and thereby suffocating it.

Despite their huge size, Burmese Pythons were readily available in the pet trade throughout the 1990's and 2000's—every pet shop that specialized in reptiles was likely to have a number of hatchling Burmese Pythons for sale. Their bright color patterns and their generally calm dispositions made them popular pets, and they were captive-bred in a variety of different color patterns and strains, including albino.

Although Burmese Pythons are generally docile and tame very readily when young, they still present dangers and difficulties to their keepers. The most dangerous time is feeding. Snakes hunt by scent, not by sight, and it's not unusual for snakes to catch the scent of a food item, see the keeper moving around, and confuse the two, striking at the keeper instead. There have been several instances in the US where large pythons mistakenly constricted and killed their keeper thinking it was a prey item—by the time the snake realized its mistake it was already too late for the keeper. It is also quite a workout just moving a large Burmese for cage-cleaning and other routine tasks. Once the snake reaches a length of 7-8 feet, it can be quite difficult for a single person to handle, particularly if that particular snake happens to be a "runner" who won't sit still. Not coincidentally, it is often right around that time that the often-inexperienced python-keeper begins to realize that perhaps keeping this species as a pet wasn't such a great idea after all.

Back in the late 90's and early 2000's, I did reptile rescue work in Florida, taking in unwanted pets, rehabilitating them, and adopting them out to new homes. Most of the calls I got were for just three species—Red-Eared Slider turtles, Green Iguanas, and Burmese Pythons. I had several dozen adult snakes pass through my hands over the years. Alas, though, there were far more unwanted pythons than there were rescuers to take them or new homes to put them in. As a result, many keepers, once they got tired of their pet, simply dumped them in a field somewhere. And there began Florida's most well-known invasive-species problem . . .

The earliest-recorded wild python in Florida was found in the Everglades in 1979. At that time, Burmese Pythons were imported mostly for zoos, and it is likely that this one was an escapee from a shipment entering the US at Miami. In the 1980's and 1990's, however, the exotic pet trade in the US expanded enormously, and numerous species of reptiles were imported in tremendous numbers, including Burmese Pythons. Released pets and escapees began showing up around virtually every Florida urban area from Tallahassee to Key West, and TV news stories regularly featured large snakes that were found in city parks or residential backyards. In areas north of Naples, the pythons were unable to survive the winter and were not able to breed in the wild. But in southern Florida, particularly in the Everglades, the conditions suited the snakes perfectly. The final blow came in 1992, when Hurricane Andrew destroyed a commercial python-breeding facility in the area, releasing dozens of captive Burmese Pythons. By 2001, the species had established a self-sustaining breeding population in the Everglades.

In desperation, the state outlawed the importation or sale of pythons and instituted a "permit" system for those already in captivity (including requirements for all snakes to be radio-chipped for identification and for keepers to submit to regular housing inspections). The

Federal government banned interstate sale of Burmese Pythons. But it was already too late. By 2005, an estimated 5,000 pythons were living in the Everglades; by 2015 estimates ranged as high as 150,000 individuals. The pythons are nocturnal hunters, and will eat virtually any mammal or bird they can catch—and will also prey on the occasional Alligator. They have measurably reduced the populations of the park's already-endangered varieties of waterbirds.

As a result, since 2005 the state has been waging an all-out war on the pythons. The Florida Fish and Wildlife Conservation Commission has a "kill on sight" policy for wild Burms, and sponsors regular "contests" for snake hunters with prizes awarded for the most snakes killed. However, the snakes are well-camouflaged, spend much of their time in the water, and are very hard to find. Fewer than a thousand pythons are killed each year—a drop in the bucket compared to the tens of thousands that are probably living and breeding in the wild. It is almost certain that the species is now firmly established and is simply impossible to eradicate.

The Red-Eared Slider

One of our most common invasives is a brightly-colored aquatic turtle called the Red-Eared Slider. Extremely common in the pet trade, the Slider has been introduced around the world, prompting some biologists to label it as "The Reptilian Norway Rat". It is listed by the International Union for the Conservation of Nature as one of the "100 Most Invasive Species in the World".

When I was a little kid in Pennsylvania, I was, like many other kids, instantly attracted to the Red-Eared Slider. With its bright green, red and yellow colors and its cute little face, baby Sliders the size of a half-dollar could be found in every Woolworth's and K-Mart, living in a tray of water with a little island and a plastic palm tree. They were sold by the thousands. Unfortunately, baby turtles are difficult to care for properly, and mine, like so many others, soon got flushed to a watery grave. But later, the relatives of these little turtles would become a scourge across the entire planet . . .

The Red-Eared Slider, also known as the Red-Eared Pond Turtle, *Trachemys scripta elegans*, is a member of the Emydid family of turtles, consisting of about 50 species known collectively as "pond turtles", "cooters" or "sliders". Most of the family is native to the Southeastern United States and Mexico. They are largely aquatic, spending their days in freshwater rivers and ponds basking onshore on rocks or logs (and dropping into the water at any disturbance), and feeding on fish and small aquatic invertebrates (many species also include aquatic plants in their diet, especially when they are adults).

Trachemys scripta elegans is a geographical subspecies of the Yellow-Bellied Slider, *T. s. scripta*. The Yellow-Bellied Slider is native to the southeastern coastal states, from southern Virginia to northern Florida, while the Red-Eared Slider is found further west in the Mississippi River Valley drainage area, from Louisiana as far north as Missouri and Illinois.

In the early 1950's, the Red-Eared Slider was introduced to the pet trade. Because the turtle breeds readily and can be easily farm-raised, millions of baby turtles flooded the market—the bright green little turtles could be found cheaply in any dime store, pet shop, and department store. Sales in the 1960's reached as high as a million a year.

As adults, they make nice pets and are relatively easy to care for, though baby turtles need special requirements like ultraviolet lighting and a calcium-rich diet. Red-Ear Sliders grow to a shell length of about ten inches. They are active swimmers, and require a large tank with an efficient filter system, as well as a large land area for basking. Sliders can live as long as 40 years.

Virtually all of the baby turtles that were being sold as pets, however, died within their first year, the victims of inadequate care. Released babies could not usually survive in the wild. Animal welfare groups, appalled by the high death rate, began lobbying for legal restrictions. By the 1970's, the fad had all but disappeared, and the number of turtles in the pet trade fell to almost nothing. In 1975, the US government, alarmed by the possibility of Salmonella transmission to humans (the bacteria are found naturally on turtle shells), finally banned the sale of baby turtles as pets.

The situation changed drastically, however, in the 1980's, when the TV show/movie "Teenage Mutant Ninja Turtles" became a smash hit. Now, turtles once again became a huge craze in the pet trade, and farm-raised adults were sold by the millions all over the world—and by now, improved knowledge about their captive care meant that a large proportion of these were surviving for many years. As children tired of their pets and parents no longer wanted to maintain the large aquariums necessary for them, adult Red-Eared Sliders began to be dumped into rivers and ponds all over the world. Unlike the rather delicate babies, adult Sliders are tough and adaptable; they soon thrived in their new wild homes.

By the early 1990's, wild non-native populations had been established in at least 23 states in the US, from California to New York and as far north as Michigan, and had also become established in Hawaii, Guam, Britain, Japan, Australia, New Zealand, South Africa, Israel, France, Canada, Germany, Bahrain, and Mexico. Some countries in Southeast Asia imported the turtle as food, not as pets, but the result was the same as escaped/released Red-Eared Sliders began to establish themselves in local waterways. By 2005, the species could be found on every continent in the world except Antarctica. Even in areas where it is too cold for the turtles to breed successfully, their populations are constantly replenished by fresh supplies of newly-released pets. By 2010, the turtle had been legally banned as an invasive species by many countries, including Australia and the European Union.

In the 1960's, some isolated populations of Red-Eared Slider were already being seen in Florida, but it wasn't until the "Ninja Turtle" craze of the 1980's that the number of Sliders exploded and the species became widely established throughout the state. By the 2000's, the non-native turtles outnumbered the native Florida Redbelly species, and the Sliders had even successfully adapted to living in salt-water bays and inlets. State officials became more alarmed when it was discovered that the introduced Red-Ear Sliders were beginning to interbreed with the native Yellow-Bellied Sliders, swamping them out genetically and endangering the entire subspecies. (Other states have faced similar problems with other members of the *Trachemys* genus.)

In 2007, Florida banned the sale of Red-Eared Sliders within the state; it is also illegal to move a Slider from one location in Florida to another or to release one. People who already have Red-Eared Sliders can keep them, but have to meet housing requirements to prevent escapes, are banned from obtaining any more, and are required to destroy any offspring. Commercial turtle breeders are still allowed to farm-raise the species, but they can only be sold out-of-state. Florida makes an exception for specially-bred "color morphs" such as albino turtles — the higher price on these, it was assumed, would make it less likely for individuals to liberate them into the wild, and the non-natural colors would reduce their chances of survival even if they were released.

So no matter what state you live in, the odds are that you will sooner or later encounter one of the "Reptilian Norway Rats".

The Lionfish

The Lionfish, also called the Turkeyfish — is an attractive and popular saltwater aquarium fish that has venomous spines on its back, breeds like a rabbit, and has an insatiable appetite for eating local fish.

There are 10 species of Lionfish in the genus *Pterois*. They are members of the Scorpaenid family, which includes about 400 species of scorpionfish, stonefish, and lionfish. Most members of the family have a series of long spines hidden inside their dorsal and pectoral fins which are connected to venom glands at the base. When the fish is stepped on or molested, the skin on the fins slides back to expose the spine, which injects venom on penetration. In several species, the venom can be lethal to humans.

The *Pterois* group is known by a variety of names—Lionfish, Turkeyfish, Dragonfish, Zebrafish, Firefish, or Butterfly Codfish. One of these species, the Red Lionfish, *Pterois volitans*, is, like the other members of the group, native to the Indo-Pacific ocean regions. With its long flowing fins and its bright contrasting brownish-red and white stripes, the Red Lionfish is extraordinarily attractive, and when the saltwater-aquarium hobby exploded in the US in the early 1980's, it quickly became popular in the pet trade and was imported from Indonesia and the Philippines in large numbers. (Even Captain Picard of the starship *Enterprise* had a Red Lionfish in his Ready Room.)

Unfortunately, many of the people who purchased the fish for their home aquariums didn't really know what they were getting into. Like most members of the Scorpionfish family, the Red Lionfish has venomous spines in its pectoral and dorsal fins. Although they are not usually fatal to humans, they can give an enormously painful sting (leading to the common name "Firefish"). The Red Lionfish can also reach a pretty large size for an aquarium fish—up to 18 inches—and has a proportionately large mouth, allowing it to eat any smaller fish that share its tank (up to two-thirds its own length). As a result, it wasn't very long before aquarium hobbyists in Florida began releasing their no-longer-wanted pets into the sea.

The first record of a Lionfish captured in Florida waters was in 1985, when a *P. volitans* (most likely a released pet) was found off the coast of Dania Beach. In 1992, Hurricane Andrew destroyed a local aquarium near Miami and released at least six captive Lionfish into the Bay of Biscayne; there were also reports that the hurricane had wrecked a number of outdoors holding tanks for tropical fish importers and released their contents. Within a few years, wild Lionfish were being sighted at Miami, Boca Raton, Palm Beach, and Bermuda, and by 2000 they had spread up the East Coast as far as North Carolina. The species reached the Bahamas by 2005 and had also spread to the Florida Keys—by 2010 they had gone all the way up the Gulf coast of Florida to the Panhandle, and south to the Caribbean and Mexico. By 2013 they had spread as far as Barbados and the coast of Venezuela. Genetic testing of captured Lionfish link them to populations in the Philippines, and indicate that the entire existing population here in the US is descended from fewer than a dozen breeding females from two distinct locations, probably escaped or released captives.

In the areas where it has been introduced, the Lionfish has no known predators. The native sharks and other predators do not recognize it as a prey species, and the venomous spines protect it from most predators who might try to sample it. The females, meanwhile, are prolific breeders. They can lay up to 30,000 eggs at a time—and usually breed every month. As a result, the Lionfish's population growth has been explosive. In some areas, the population of wild *Pterois volitans* was observed to increase by over seven times in just four years; their population density in areas where they have been introduced is over ten times as large as in their native ranges in the Pacific.

In such densities, the fish have an enormous impact on local ecosystems. Lionfish are voracious feeders, and will happily eat any fish they can fit in their mouths— and a single adult Lionfish can eat as many as 20 smaller reef fish in half an hour. Not only do they devastate the numbers of small native reef fish, but they compete for food with larger fish such as grouper and snapper, reducing those populations as well. In many areas, Lionfish infestations have reduced local species, in both number and diversity, by over 50%, and have established themselves as the most abundant fish. One study demonstrated that Lionfish can reduce the number of smaller fish in the area by 80% in just five weeks. Officials at NOAA, the US Fish and Wildlife Service, and state environmental agencies all along the US east coast consider the Lionfish to be the single largest threat to our native marine reef environments. Most coastal states are funding frantic scientific studies of the fish in the wild, hoping to find some vulnerability or some effective method of control.

But because of their prolific breeding rate and their invulnerability to predators, Florida Fish and Wildlife officials have pretty much given up any hope of eradicating the species (it has been estimated that removing the species totally would require killing them at the rate of at least 25% of the entire population of Lionfish every month). So the goal right now is to attempt to cull as many of them as possible to try to keep their population densities at a tolerable level. Research is being undertaken to develop a fish trap that targets the Lionfish. The fish have no legal protections whatsoever, and fishermen and divers are also being heartily encouraged by the state to kill as many of them as possible. All along the coasts of Florida, periodic

"Lionfish Hunts" are organized for divers and fishermen, with prizes awarded for the most Lionfish killed. These outings can remove as many as 5-6,000 fish at a time.

In another creative tactic, Florida officials attempted to make up for the Lionfish's lack of predators by turning Florida's citizens themselves into predators, by commissioning the writing of a number of cookbooks with Lionfish recipes (the fish have a delicate light edible flesh similar to grouper that is highly prized by those who have tried it; though the venomous spines can make catching them a bit hazardous, the venom itself is destroyed by cooking). The hope is that commercial fisheries and restaurants will develop a thriving industry around the fish, thereby turning the invaders into an economic asset while removing them from the reefs. A number of fisheries in Key West are already marketing the Lionfish they accidentally catch in their lobster traps to high-end seafood restaurants in New York and Miami. One difficulty with the "catch and eat" management strategy, however, is that the Lionfish like to lurk near the bottom in shallow water, which makes it hard to net them in commercial numbers—as a result, they are usually caught by spearfishers, which makes them rather expensive.

Can human predators become an effective check to the Lionfish invasion? It remains to be seen . . .

The Water Hyacinth

One of our plant invaders is a free-floating aquatic plant with showy violet-blue flowers, the Water Hyacinth. Its aggressive invasiveness have led biologists to label it "the worst plant in the world".

The Water Hyacinth, *Eichhornia crassipes*, is in the family Pontederiaceae, which includes other aquatic plants such as Pickerelweed and the Mud Plantains. It is native to Brazil. Unlike Pickerelweeds, which root themselves in the mud at the shoreline, Water Hyacinth is free-floating, consisting of wide rosettes of thick round or fan-shaped leaves, each leafstalk with a bulbous swelling near the base that provides flotation. The feathery roots dangle into the water, and the violet-blue flowers bloom on stalks that can extend as much as three feet above the plant. Water Hyacinth is the fastest-reproducing plant that has ever been measured — in addition to seeds, the plant can reproduce asexually by sending out horizontal runners called "stolons" which produce daughter plants. A single plant is capable of producing as many as 600 offspring within four months. A patch of Water Hyacinth can easily double its size in less than two weeks, and form thick dense mats in which most of the individual plants are linked to each other through stolons.

Because of its free-floating lifestyle and its attractive foliage and flowers, Water Hyacinth has long been popular for use as an ornamental plant in water gardens, fish ponds and aquariums, and has been widely exported around the world (many Internet aquarium shops sell it). As a result, it is one of the most common invasive plants on earth, and has now been established in over 50 countries in Africa, Asia and Australia. In the US, Water Hyacinth has become introduced throughout the Southeast, from North Carolina to Texas, and also in southern California and Hawaii. The plants have also been found in the wild in New York, Tennessee, Kentucky, Washington, Missouri, Arkansas and Oregon, but because the tropical Water Hyacinth cannot tolerate cold temperatures, they cannot survive the winter in these northern areas.

Once it becomes established, the plant can quickly cover an entire body of water, from shore to shore. The dense mats block out sunlight, killing off most of the native aquatic plants. They also reduce oxygen levels in the water, which can kill fish and other aquatic life. One acre of Water Hyacinth plants can weigh over 200 tons, enough to interfere with boats (making many rivers un-navigable) and to choke off water flow, turning the water stagnant. It also deposits about 500 tons of dead and rotted plant material on the bottom each year, leading to ponds and waterways being filled in.

It is believed that Water Hyacinth first entered Florida in 1884, by way of New Orleans. In 1884, at the New Orleans World Fair, a pavilion from Japan was giving out free Water Hyacinths as ornamental water plants (why the Japanese were giving out a plant from Brazil is a question that can no longer be answered.) One of the visitors to the World's Fair was Mrs WF Fuller from Florida, who took the lovely little plant with her back to Palatka, on the St John's River, and put it in her outdoors fish pond. When a sheet of Water Hyacinth covered her pond, she thinned it out, tossing some extra plants around her boat dock on the St John's River. By 1896, the plant covered more than 200 miles of river. When rancher Eli Morgan saw how quickly the plant grew, he in turn decided it would make a good food source for his cattle, and transferred some Water Hyacinths to his ranch on the Kissimmee River. As it turned out, Water Hyacinths aren't very nutritious and the cattle didn't like them anyway. But the plants soon spread along the Kissimmee, reaching Lake Okeechobee and fanning out across southern Florida. By the 1960's, Water Hyacinth mats covered some 120,000 acres of ponds and rivers all over Florida.

The state launched a multi-million dollar campaign to eradicate the invader. The plant was made illegal to import, keep, or release. Waterborne machines were developed to grind the mats into pulp, and large amounts of plant poisons were sprayed onto them. In some areas, two species of Hyacinth Weevils, insects from Brazil that kill the plants, were released as a form of biological control. Although reduced by over 98%, however, the plant defied all efforts to eradicate it. Today, Florida uses a constant program of "maintenance control" to keep the invasive plant at a tolerable level.

The Brown Anole

Every tourist has seen these ubiquitous little lizards running along sidewalks, tree trunks, or fences, conspicuously bobbing their heads and displaying their brightly-colored extendable throat fan at each other.

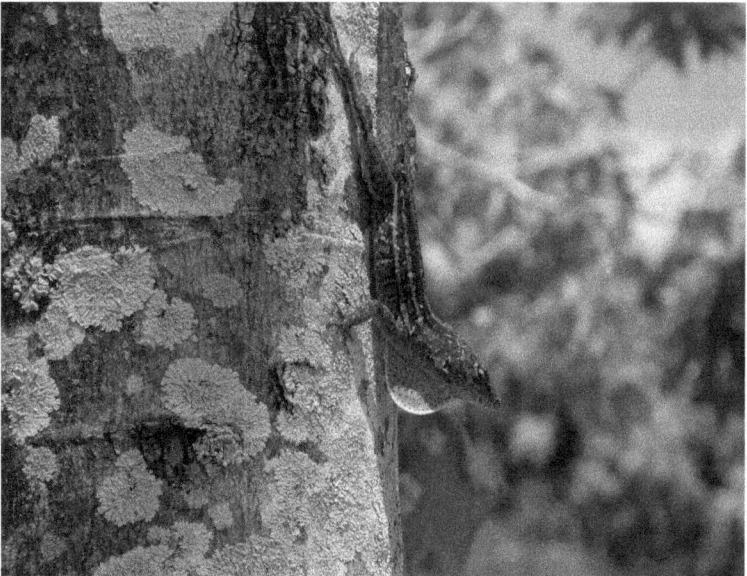

There are about 400 different species of Anole lizards, all of them found in the tropical Americas. Taxonomically, they have been recently moved from the Iguanid family into a new family of their own, the Polychrotids. *Anolis* contains the largest number of species of any vertebrate genus. A proposal has been made (but not yet widely accepted) to separate about 150 of these and place them into their own genus, *Norops*. Among these proposed species is *Anolis (Norops) sagrei*, the Brown Anole.

The Brown Anole is just a little fellow, not more than seven or eight inches from nose to tail. Native to Cuba, and found as a subspecies in the Bahamas and several other Caribbean islands, it was first described scientifically in 1837. It is a brownish-tan color, lighter at the sides and darker on the back, though like most members of the *Anolis* group it can change its skin color, usually according to temperature—pale brown when warm, and darker brown to almost black when cool. Like all reptiles, the lizards are cold-blooded, and darker colors help them absorb more heat from the sun.

The females have a light-colored zigzag stripe along their back. The much larger males have faint vertical rows of light-colored spots on their sides, an erectable crest running down their neck and back, and also have a large dewlap under their chin, brightly colored yellow-orange or reddish. They are fiercely territorial, and males spend much of their time patrolling their turf, head-bobbing and displaying their dewlaps to each other as a warning.

As with many lizards, Brown Anoles have the ability to voluntarily cast off their own tails, known as "autotomy". If seized by a predator, the lizard can break off its own tail, which then twitches spasmodically and distracts the attacker while the lizard escapes. Although the tail eventually grows back, it's not unusual to see

Brown Anoles with half their tail missing. They are insectivores, and eat any sort of small arthropod that they can catch. In captivity they can live as long as 6 or 7 years, but in the wild they seldom live more than 18 months.

Another member of the genus is *Anolis carolinensis*, the Green Anole. Generally a bit smaller in size than the Brown Anole, the Green Anole is found throughout the southeastern US, from Texas to North Carolina — the only *Anolis* native to the US. Because it can change its skin color from green to brown, it is also known as the American Chameleon (though it is not related to the true chameleons from Madagascar). From the 1950's on, it was very commonly sold in pet stores. And, as it turns out, many imported Brown Anoles were also sold as pets. And there begins our problem . . .

The first recorded sighting of a Brown Anole in Florida was way back in 1887, in the Keys. Very likely, the lizards had been reaching Florida for millennia, rafting over on floating driftwood or trees that were blown to the mainland during hurricanes. During this time, the Brown Anoles were not able to successfully compete with the native Green Anoles, and were never able to establish themselves.

By the 1940's, however, circumstances had changed. The human population of Florida surged, and large cities appeared on both coasts. These suburban areas provided wonderful habitat for introduced lizards. By the 1950's, wild Brown Anoles were being reported in several cities in southern Florida, and by 1980, they could be found throughout most of the state. Originally there were two distinct subspecies present, the Cuban Anole *Anolis sagrei sagrei*, and the Bahaman Anole *Anolis sagrei ordinatus*. But in Florida they have now interbred so much that the *ordinatus* subspecies is no longer recognizable. They do not seem to interbreed with the native *Anolis carolinensis*.

The establishment of the Brown Anole invaders had an immediate effect on the native Greens. While the Green Anole is largely arboreal and prefers high branches with lots of foliage in forested areas, the Brown Anole is largely terrestrial, spending most of its time on the ground and on the bare lower branches and trunks of trees and bushes. It particularly likes open shrubby areas — such as urban parks and suburban lawns. With its higher birth rate (and its larger size), the Brown Anole was able to quickly push the native Green out of the urban areas, and the Green Anoles retreated to the remaining forested tracts in Florida where the Browns preferred not to go (the arboreal Green Anoles are apparently better able than the ground-dwelling Brown Anoles to avoid predators in forested areas). Today, it's rare to see a native Green Anole in the city, and the Brown Anoles have completely taken over. From Florida, they have advanced into southern Georgia. Being less cold-tolerant than the native Green Anoles, this may be as far as the Browns can go.

The Black-Hooded Parakeet

The Black-Hooded Parakeet is also known as the Nanday Parakeet or the Nanday Conure. A small parrot, Aratinga nanday is native to Brazil, Paraguay and Argentina. Its diminutive size, its brash personality and its high intelligence have made it a favorite in the pet trade – and that's how it got here.

It's not known exactly how and where the Black-Hooded Parakeet entered Florida. The initial reports happened in 1969 and centered around the Tampa Bay and Miami-Dade areas. Both of these cities have ports which are major hubs for the exotic-pet import industry, so it's conceivable that a shipment of birds could have escaped from either one of these areas, or both. In other counties, it is possible that the birds were introduced independently, by escaped or released pets. By the 1990's, colonies of Black-Hooded Parakeets were being reported in ten Florida counties; today they have been found in at least 19 counties. In ten of these, including Pinellas County (St Petersburg area) and Miami, they are known to be breeding. In those areas of Florida where they are not observed to be breeding in the wild, it is presumed that the group is maintained by continuous replenishment through escapes/released pets. Individual birds can live as long as 25 years.

The birds have also established colonies, through escapes/releases, in other areas. There are breeding colonies of free-living Black-Hooded Parakeets in Hawaii, Puerto Rico, San Antonio TX, and in several areas of California, including Los Angeles and Sacramento. Non-breeding groups have been seen in New York City.

There is no missing a flock of Black-Hooded Parakeets. The birds are about a foot tall with a two-foot wingspan, and travel low to the ground in flocks of 20-30. The bright electric-green body with bluish breast and jet-black hood and beak make them conspicuous and unmistakable, but their loud raucous continuous calls and piercing squawks usually mean you can hear them long before you can see them.

Urban Florida is a perfect habitat for the birds. In the wild, they feed on seeds, palm fruits, and flower buds, and prefer habitats at the edges of clearings and in open grasslands. Urban areas, with their parks and suburban lawns, suit them wonderfully. They nest in tree cavities, and have broods of three or four at a time. In their native wild, they are one of the few parrot species that are not in environmental danger.

So what is the State of Florida planning to do about the uninvited guests? There's nothing it *can* do. The birds are already widely established and already breeding. It is expected that eventually they will spread to cover the entire state.

The Love Bugs

If you are in Florida long enough, especially in spring or autumn, you'll probably hear the whispered legend of the Love Bugs and how they are escapees from a mysterious genetic lab experiment. The truth though is more mundane – the Love Bugs are just another of Florida's invaders.

The Love Bug, scientific name *Plecia nearctica*, is a member of the Bibionidae family of flies, which are related to the mosquitoes, midges, and gnats. Some other common names for them include March Flies, Honeymoon Bugs, Double-Headed Bugs, and United Flies—but by far the most well-known name is "Love Bugs". In appearance, they are small, less than half an inch in length, with the female a bit larger than the male. Like all flies, they have a single pair of wings. The body and wings are jet black, and the thorax, where the wings attach, is bright red. The red is a warning color—although they cannot bite or sting, the adults have acidic chemicals in their bodies that make most birds sick if they eat them (though a few species can tolerate the chemicals and happily snap them up).

For most of the time, Love Bugs are inoffensive critters that spend nearly their entire lives as a larva, happily munching on rotted plant material on the ground. The larvae take several months to reach sexual maturity, when they molt a final time, pupate, and emerge as a winged adult—then take to the air to find a mate.

In Florida, we get two crops of adult Love Bugs each year, once in May and again in September. (Down near Miami in warm years we may also get a third crop, in late December.) During these mating seasons, the Love Bugs emerge in swarms of thousands. The adults only live for a few days, and have just a short time to find a mate and breed before they die. And that leads to the plague, as constant swarms of Love Bugs, joined together abdomen to abdomen, fly around aimlessly in the throes of passion. The larger female drags the hapless male around through the air, backwards. Many of them will hook up, land, and lay eggs inside a plant stem for the next generation. Many more, however, will get splattered by cars, or get swatted when they fly into the faces and hair of annoyed humans. They land on beach-goers and get stuck in their suntan oil; they flop helplessly into your drink or your lunch if you eat outside. Swarms are often so thick that they can cover car windshields with smooshed slime, or even clog radiators and make the car overheat. And the acid in their blood has the added feature of eating the paint off your car. For about three weeks, the things are absolutely everywhere and fly into absolutely everything.

Until the 1950's, there weren't even any Love Bugs in Florida, and car paintjobs and uncovered Mai Tai's were safe from the scourge. This sudden appearance has led to the widespread urban legend in Florida that the Love Bug is actually a man-made creation. In the early 1950's, the story goes, researchers at the University of Florida in Gainesville were looking for a way to control Florida's mosquito population, and hit upon the idea of producing something that would be sterile but would breed with the female mosquitoes, making them produce infertile eggs. By crossbreeding a species of fly with a mosquito (and perhaps by genetically engineering the resulting hybrid), the scientists, the story goes, produced the Love Bug. But, through some accident, the GMO bugs escaped into the wild, where, in the absence of natural predators, they reproduced wildly and went beyond control, giving us our present-day twice-yearly plague.

It's a great story, but alas it is simply not true. Love Bugs are actually a quite normal species of fly which is native to Central America. Somehow or another, they made their way to New Orleans in the 1920's (they may have stowed away on a boat, or they may have migrated naturally along the Gulf Coast of Mexico), and from there they spread out into Texas, Alabama, Mississippi,

Georgia and Florida, reaching us in the 1950's just as Florida's human population was beginning to explode. The conditions in Florida seem to particularly suit them, and we seem to have the heaviest populations. Lucky us.

The Starling

One of our invaders – the European Starling – is said to be all William Shakespeare's fault.

In 1854, the prominent French biologist Isidore Geoffroy Saint-Hilaire helped organize a group in Paris that called itself the "Society for Acclimatisation", which had as its stated goal the introduction and establishment of plants and animals into France from around the world, "such as may be useful or desirable". Within a few years, similar societies appeared around the world. They were particularly popular in colonial regions, where homesick Europeans embraced the idea of bringing in familiar plants and animals to make them feel more at home. While the idea of deliberately bringing in non-native wildlife may strike us today as odd or even dangerous, the Europeans knew nothing of the hazards of introduced species, and the practice reflected the political and social ideas of their time, that European culture (in all its aspects) was superior to the wild savagery of the rest of the world and that it was a service to humanity to bring "Europe" everywhere. "Acclimatisation Societies" appeared across the world, from England to Australia, and in 1871 the American Acclimatisation Society was founded in New York City by the wealthy medical-drug manufacturer Eugene Schieffelin.

Previous efforts had already been made to bring a little bit of Europe to the Americas. In the 1850's, the commissioners of Central Park had imported and released English Sparrows, Chinese Pheasants, Skylarks and European Robins, with the aim of "improving the beauty" of the park. (The Sparrows and the Pheasants were spectacularly successful, and now inhabit most of the US.)

Schieffelin, an enthusiastic student of English literature, is said to have brought an odd twist to the story, however, when he convinced the Acclimatisation Society to introduce every species of bird that was mentioned in the complete plays of William Shakespeare. In the Bard's historical play *Henry IV*, the character Hotspur proclaims of the King, "I will have a starling shall be taught to speak nothing but 'Mortimer,' and give it him, to keep his anger still in motion." In 1890 and 1891, the Society released approximately 100 European Starlings into Central Park.

The Starling (*Sturnus vulgaris*) is common in Europe. About the size of a robin, it is a strikingly handsome bird — dark blue or black with white feather tips that give it the appearance of a starry sky, hence its name. Starlings travel and feed in large raucous flocks. They are accomplished mimics, and captives have been taught to talk — which is why it appears in Shakespeare's play.

The birds need trees with cavities for nesting and grassy open areas to forage for insects and seeds, and therefore suburban lawns and city parks suit them perfectly. Within a few decades, the Starlings released in Central Park had spread outwards, and eventually covered the entire country. The first record in Florida is a Starling captured in Jacksonville in 1918; they had reached southern Florida by 1950. Today there are an estimated 200 million Starlings in the US. The species has also been deliberately introduced into Australia, South Africa, Jamaica, and New Zealand — usually as a way to control agricultural insect pests.

The Starlings compete with native birds for food supplies. They also monopolize many of the suitable locations for nest cavities. In areas with large flocks, the blanket of highly-acidic bird droppings can kill trees, damage buildings, and wreck the paint on parked cars. Flocks that gather in the open areas of airports are one of the leading causes of bird strikes. Starlings are now on the International Union for the Conservation of Nature list of "The 100 Worst Invasive Species".

If Shakespeare had known of the ecological damage he inadvertently caused, perhaps Hotspur would have given King Henry a parrot instead.

The Hydrilla

The aquatic plant Hydrilla came to us via the aquarium trade. It is listed as one of the "100 Most Invasive Species in the World" and has been called "The Perfect Aquatic Weed".

Hydrilla verticillata is the only member of its genus. It is part of the Hydrocharitaceae family, known as "Frog-Bits". The species was first described by Linneaus in 1782 from specimens found in Europe. By that time it was already found in most of the warm parts of Africa and Asia, and was so widespread that today no one is even certain where it originally evolved (most guesses center around southern Asia). The plant prefers warm tropical conditions, but it is also capable of surviving and reproducing in cooler temperate areas. In addition, it can tolerate brackish water and survive in tidal estuaries.

In appearance, Hydrilla consists of long jointed stems, often multi-branched, with a series of 7 or 8 small leaflets arranged in circular whorls along their lengths and a dense growth bud at the tip. It is entirely aquatic, capable of thriving in any permanent body of freshwater, even just a few inches deep. The plant is widely variable and has several different patterns of growth. In many cases, Hydrilla forms small tubers in the bottom mud, up to a foot deep, from which the stems can reach as long as 25 feet to the surface. When rooted, the bare stems reach up to the surface, where they then branch out extensively, forming a thick layer and putting over 80% of the plant's mass at the water surface. The tubers also put out subterranean runners to make new stems.

In many areas, though, the tubers can be dispensed with entirely, and the long branched stems simply float freely at the surface. Any fragments of stem that break off will grow into an entirely new plant. And finally, some forms of Hydrilla can also reproduce from seed—its flowers are tiny and inconspicuous. Two different forms of Hydrilla are found in the US—the most common form contains only female flowers and cannot produce seeds. But an isolated population in North Carolina contains both male and female flowers—it is assumed that this variety has a different source than the more common type, and that there have been invasions by this plant from at least two different geographic areas.

In good environmental conditions, Hydrilla can grow as fast as a full inch per day. Even just a few fragments of stem are capable of completely overgrowing a body of water within a few months, forming a tangled mat floating on the surface. The thick mats choke off water flow and can be so heavy that they stop boat traffic. Growths of Hydrilla also shade out other plants, deplete the oxygen level in the water, and rapidly fill in ponds and lakes with thick sediment layers of dead plant material.

Hydrilla's attractive feathery appearance and deep green color, and its ease of propagation, made it a favorite with home aquarium hobbyists, and in the 1950's and 1960's the plant was widely sold in pet stores and specialist aquarium shops, often labeled as "Elodea" or "Anacharis". As a result, it quickly became established in Australia, South America, and the US. Its first appearance in the US happened in Florida in 1960, when wild colonies were found in the Crystal River area near Tampa and in a canal near Miami. By the early 1990's Hydrilla had infested almost half of the lakes in the entire state and covered over 140,000 acres of water surface, and had spread throughout the southeast up to Maryland, and in the west-coast states of California and Washington. It was even found in ponds and lakes in Arizona, presumably released by aquarium keepers. In the US, the Hydrilla invasion has so far not spread to most of the northern states, but in other countries like Russia and Poland, the plant has established itself in conditions similar to those at the US-Canada border. It is therefore likely that Hydrilla will continue to spread until it occupies the entire US.

Florida promptly banned import or possession of the plant, but it was already too late. Once Hydrilla establishes itself in a body of water, it can produce several thousand submerged tubers per acre, which are impossible to eradicate. The state estimates that at least 40,000 acres of wetland are still occupied by Hydrilla growth. Florida spends around $20 million a year to try to control the plant, mostly with herbicides. Grass Carp eat Hydrilla in large quantities—but Grass Carp are themselves an invasive species and are illegal to introduce in most states (including Florida). State officials have carried out some experiments in using sterilized Grass Carp as a method of controlling Hydrilla in individual bodies of water.

Hydrilla does have one potential bright side, though. It is very efficient at extracting nutrients, and it has been seriously considered as a form of bio-remediation for filtering and cleaning toxic levels of heavy metals from polluted bodies of water.

The Giant African Land Snail

One of our most recent invaders is a giant snail that will not only eat your yard, but your house, too.

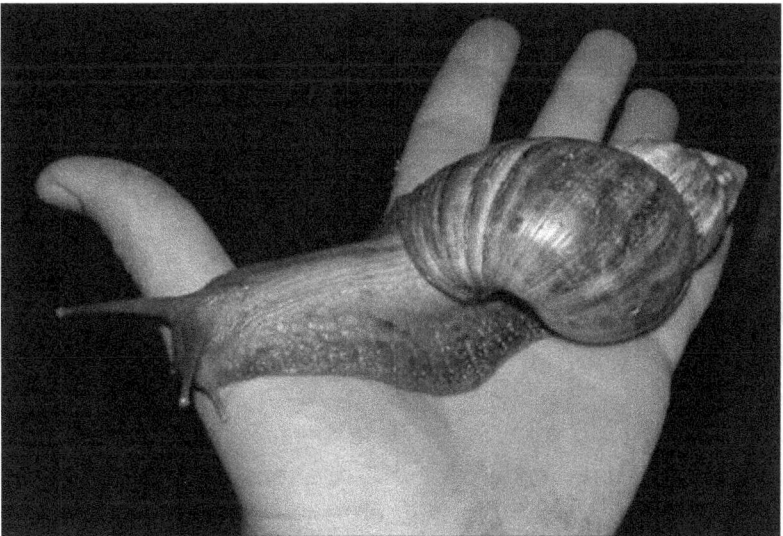

The Giant African Land Snail (GALS, for short) lives up to its name. The cone-shaped spiral shell is fist-sized, and the snail within can measure over eight inches, making it one of the largest land snails in the world. *Achatina fulica* (some authorities classify it in the genus *Lissachatina* instead) is one of three species of giant land snail. Native to Tanzania and Kenya, these huge mollusks are plant-eaters, feeding on live or dead vegetation. To obtain the calcium they require for their shells, they will also eat pebbles, animal bones, cement, or the plaster stucco from houses.

Like most snails, GALS are hermaphrodites — that is, each individual has both male and female sex organs. When breeding, two individuals that are about the same size will fertilize each other, and both will then lay eggs. If the snails are unequal in size, the smaller one will fertilize the larger, who will play the role of the female. The courtship display involves lots of head-rubbing and neck-twining. Each clutch can contain two hundred eggs, laid every two months, and youngsters can reach sexual maturity in five months. Adults can live up to nine years.

The Giant African Land Snail can survive virtually anywhere where warm and humid conditions can be found. They are mostly nocturnal and spend the day buried in the ground to conserve moisture. In dry times of the year, the snails secrete a calcareous plug for their shell that seals them in and prevents them from drying out.

From the early 1900s, GALS were imported and farmed as a food source, which had led to its escape and introduction as an invasive. One of the first places invaded was Nigeria, where the *Achatina* snails crowded out most of the native snail species. By 1936, the Giant African Snails had become established in China, Taiwan, and several Pacific islands, including Hawaii. The Second World War helped spread the snails, both by shipping them as food for troops, and by moving unseen stowaways. Several native religious sects, including Santeria and Candomble, also use the snail in ceremonies and rituals. Religious groups have inadvertently introduced escapees into Brazil and the Caribbean islands. In the early 2000's, the snails were briefly popular in the exotic pet trade, especially as classroom display animals, and although the US (and most other countries) has passed laws banning their import or possession, some number of snails are still being illegally smuggled into the US as pets each year. Today invasive populations are found all over Africa, South America, Asia and Australia.

Once established, the snails become serious agricultural pests. They are listed as one of the "100 Worst Invasives".

Florida's first encounter with the Giant African Land Snail was in 1966, when a young boy who visited his grandmother in Hawaii brought three snails home with him to Miami and released them in his backyard. Within five years there were thousands of them spread over miles, and the state embarked on a million-dollar eradication effort that eventually took ten years, but succeeded—the only time on record that a GALS infestation was successfully removed.

But in September 2011, the snails were back again, now in the Coral Gables area. No one is sure how they got there this time—it may have been from illegal pets, or it may have been an escape from a local Santeria group that was found using the snails in its rituals. In any case, the snails have bred rapidly. Though so far they are limited to a small geographic area in Dade County, state officials have already removed and killed over 130,000 individual snails. They have been found at densities of over 2,000 individuals per square mile. A team of snail-hunters from Florida's Department of Agriculture (they have a staff of 40 people devoted to eradicating the snails) uses traps, poison-bait, and specially-trained sniffing dogs to find the mollusks. (The poisons don't work so well—the snails, like rats, are able to learn if they get sick from eating something and won't eat it again.)

Unlike most invasive species, however, this one is a fight that Florida seems to be winning. Thanks to the massive eradication effort, the GALS invasion has remained confined to a small geographic area, and their numbers seem to be declining.

The Green Iguana

It's one of the largest lizards in the world, and the largest in the Western Hemisphere. It was one of the most popular reptile pets of all time. And now it has invaded Florida. It's the Green Iguana.

The Iguanas are a widespread group of lizards, ranging from North and South America all the way to the Pacific islands and Madagascar. The "true Iguanas" are in a subfamily known as Iguaninae, which includes the Chuckwalla and Desert Iguanas of the Southwest US, the Spinytail Iguanas of Mexico and Central America, the Rock Iguanas or Rhinoceros Iguanas of the Caribbean, the Land Iguana and Marine Iguana of the Galapagos Islands, and the Fijian Iguana in the Pacific. It also includes the Green Iguana, which is the most common and widespread species, ranging from Mexico and the Caribbean through Central America to southern Brazil. The scientific name, conveniently enough, is *Iguana iguana*. The name "iguana" comes from the word that the Caribbean Island natives used to refer to these lizards—*iwana*. Green iguanas reach an adult length of six feet, and can live up to 15 years.

The widespread Green Iguanas can vary noticeably in color according to their geographic location. In general, Iguanas from the northern parts of their range, like Mexico, tend to be orangish in hue, while those from the southernmost parts of their habitat, Peru or Brazil, tend towards a bluish-gray color. Central American Iguanas are usually bright green. The colors on an individual Iguana can also change according to its mood. When cold or very frightened, Iguanas tend to darken their colors. Conversely, they tend to look paler if they are too warm or if they are vigorously making a threat display. During breeding season, male Iguanas reinforce their territorial displays with a wash of bright orange or rust color on their head and neck. During a territorial display, the dark crossbands on the Iguana's tail and body often become more vivid. Normally, these bars provide camouflage in the dappled shadows of the forest canopy. Male Iguanas spend a lot of time defending their territory from each other, warning each other away with a display of head-bobbing and dewlap-extending. In general, young

Iguanas throughout their range tend to be a much brighter and more vivid green than their adult relatives. As they get older, their color patterns tend to fade.

In the wild, the preferred habitat of the Green Iguana is lush tropical forest along river-courses. They are almost completely arboreal and only occasionally descend to the ground, though they often drop into water from overhanging branches if disturbed — they are excellent swimmers, though their long climbing toes make them awkward walkers on land.

Iguanas are unusual among reptiles in being almost completely vegetarian, feeding entirely on plant material (occasional reports have them eating bird eggs, however). Even among herbivorous animals, Green Iguanas have their particular niche virtually to themselves. Although many other animals live in the rainforest canopy, only Iguanas and a few specialized monkeys are able to subsist on a steady diet of mature tree leaves. Other arboreal herbivores cannot deal with the tough fibrous leaves, and instead focus on the fruits or the tender new leaves and shoots, which are much easier to digest. The Iguana uses commensual bacteria in its gut to break down the tough cellulose into usable sugars. Because their diet consists largely of tree leaves, Iguanas can only survive in areas where there are large amounts of foliage year-round — and that means tropical areas.

In the wild, Iguanas are semi-social animals. Although they live in groups and are only seldom found alone, these aggregations are not very closely-knit, and are not true social groups like a pride of lions or a troop of baboons would be. Most individual Iguanas, particularly the females, may enter or leave a particular group at whim, and individual animals in a group may or may not be related to each other. A consistent trend, though, is that Iguanas of the same age and size tend to hang around together. It is rare to see younger, smaller Iguanas sharing a space with larger adults—partly because younger Iguanas are suited to a different ecological "micro-habitat" than are adults (preferring low shrubs and bushes rather than trees), and partly because the larger adults would make it a habit to push around and intimidate the youngsters if they were together.

A great proportion of the scattered islands in the Caribbean have been colonized by Iguanas. Although biologists had long suspected that the Iguanas reached these isolated islands by floating there, they were unable to directly observe an instance of that happening until 1995, when hurricanes Luis and Marilyn followed each other through the Caribbean within two weeks. During the storms, a huge mat of logs and mud was dislodged from the island of Guadeloupe and floated away on the sea. Perched atop it were at least 15 Green Iguanas of various sizes and ages. Three weeks later, the raft washed ashore at the previously iguana-free island of Anguilla, over 175 miles away, and the Iguanas, who had survived their journey without any access to food or water, found a new home. Today their descendants are still breeding on Anguilla.

It is likely that Green Iguanas were floating to Florida for thousands of years in this same manner, though they apparently never became established here—until they got some help from humans . . .

In the early 1980's, the reptile pet trade in the United States exploded, and the Green Iguana was at the top of the list. The species was already being commercially farmed in Central America as a food animal (people there call it "tree chicken"), so it wasn't long before huge numbers of hatchling baby Iguanas began arriving in the US for the pet trade, as many as 800,000 a year. The baby iggies were small, adorably cute, and dirt cheap—as little as ten bucks. Children everywhere in the US eagerly snapped them up.

Unfortunately, virtually none of the people who bought these baby Iguanas knew what they were getting into. Green Iguanas do not make good pets for most people. Not only do they get enormously large and require huge cages and specialized equipment (such as ultraviolet lamps and basking lights), but if they are not properly tamed and socialized as babies, they grow up to be hostile, defensive, hissing and biting demons. Trust me, being near a huge lizard that doesn't like people (and has over 100 razor-sharp teeth in its mouth as well as a tail whip that can break skin) is no fun. Of the several million Green Iguanas that were imported into the US, nearly all of them were dead within a year, the victim of improper care and unsuitable diet or conditions. Most of the survivors were ultimately released into the wild by keepers who no longer wanted them, either because they were afraid of the lizard, or couldn't provide the space needed by a six-foot pet.

Wild Green Iguanas began appearing in small numbers around Miami in 1964. It is not known if these were escaped/released pets, refugees from exotic animal shipments at the port of Miami, or stragglers that had rafted in from the Caribbean islands. But by 1990, the pet trade in these lizards was thriving, and they began appearing all over Florida. (Two other species, the Black Spinytail Iguana and the Mexican Spinytail Iguana, also became popular in the pet trade and made their way to Florida). In most of the state, these invaders could not survive the winter (though in some areas like Tampa Bay, new escapees replenished the wild population each spring and summer). But in Miami, Ft Lauderdale and the Keys, the big lizards became firmly established and began breeding, digging deep nesting holes in the sand and laying as many as 60 eggs at a time. Estimates of the number of Green Iguanas in Florida have ranged from 100,000 to 300,000. Green Iguanas have also become established in Hawaii (where they were smuggled in illegally—Hawaii has strict laws against any reptile import) and in Texas.

As invaders go, the Green Iguanas are actually pretty benign. They are vegetarian and do not prey on any of Florida's native animals or compete with them for food. They are not aggressive towards humans or other animals (though they will defend themselves vigorously with bites and tail-lashes if they are caught or cornered). Some Floridians have simply accepted the Iguanas as a new exotic addition to life in the Sunshine State. But many other residents resent the big green lizards, partly because they are afraid of them, and partly because Iguanas are eating machines and can very effectively destroy the nicest of landscaped gardens and lawns, by eating the vegetation (they are especially fond of Hibiscus and Mango trees) and by excavating their large nest pits in the ground. Some cities, like Key West, take a mostly live-and-let-live view of the lizards, while other areas have a kill-on-sight policy. The state of Florida still does not ban the sale of Iguanas, though it does forbid releasing them into the wild or moving them from one location to another. (Most pet store chains have voluntarily stopped selling baby iguanas in its stores, nationwide, citing environmental and animal-welfare concerns.)

In the winter of 2010 the Iguana invaders were dealt a severe blow, when Florida experienced an unusually cold winter—for nearly two weeks, temperatures were as much as 20 degrees below normal. The lizards cannot tolerate conditions like that, and numbed Green Iguanas, paralyzed by the cold, tumbled out of trees and onto lawns and sidewalks. Most of them died. But a number of them hung on, coming out of their torpor and reviving once temperatures returned to normal. While many areas of Florida were virtually iguana-free for a few years afterwards, by 2015 the populations were already starting to recover, and wild-born baby iguanas could be seen in many areas. It is likely that the Green Iguana is here to stay.

The Cane Toad

The Cane Toad, from South America, is the largest toad species in the world. It also packs a wallop – the poisons produced in the toad's paratoid glands are powerful enough to kill dogs.

In the early 1920's, the US Army Corps of Engineers, at the request of Florida's state government, began a massive decade-long program of excavation and drainage, digging a number of crisscrossing canals to drain away the Everglades and turn the "worthless swampland" into productive agricultural area. One of the people attracted to the new land was Charles Stewart Mott, a former General Motors executive who now owned the US Sugar Company. US Sugar set up plantations all over south Florida, encouraged and supported by generous tax breaks and subsidies from the State and Federal governments, and other sugar companies soon followed. In the 1930's, "King Sugar" quickly came to dominate the state, economically and politically.

But the industry had difficulties. Sugar cane does not grow naturally in Florida, and the climate is not really suited for it. As a result, the sugar plantations required massive amounts of fertilizers to keep the cane alive. The plantations were also infested with insect pests, and chief among these were the "white worms", the grub larvae of several species of scarab beetle. In 1932, the sugar industry in Hawaii had faced the same problem, and dealt with it by "natural pest control"—they imported 150 Giant Toads from South America (then known as *Bufo marinus*, now known as *Rhinella marina*) and released them, hoping they would eat the beetles and control the larvae.

The Giant Toad, also known as the Marine Toad or the Giant Bufo (and now known worldwide as the Cane Toad) is the largest species of toad in the world. It is found mostly in South and Central America, though native populations reach through Mexico into the southern part of Texas. In the southern tropical parts of its range the toad can reach sizes up to a foot long and weigh as much as 5 pounds. In the northern extremes of their introduced range (Texas and Florida) they get about half that size. Voracious feeders, they will swallow anything that moves that is smaller than they are.

By 1938, the toads had also been introduced into sugar plantations in the Caribbean, Louisiana, Puerto Rico, the Philippines, Australia and New Guinea. In 1936, it was Florida's turn. The University of Florida obtained 200 Giant Toads from Puerto Rico and released them at its Agricultural Experiment Station in Palm Beach County. The experiment failed when nearly all the toads died. So a few years later, two sugar companies in Glades County and Dade County tried again, releasing several hundred toads. Alas, the toads did not make any significant impact on the beetle populations, and most of them died out too. The sugar industry gave up, and used a plethora of pesticides on its cane fields instead.

In 1955, however, the toads got a lucky break. A shipment of Cane Toads that had been imported from Colombia was sitting on the tarmac at Miami Airport when the crate was accidentally broken open, and 100 toads went hopping off to freedom. This time, the population managed to establish itself. In 1958, a new canal was dug which connected the breeding ponds being used by the toads to the rest of South Florida's extensive canal system, and the toads were free to move. By the 1970's they had covered most of southern Florida, and by the 80's they had reached Tampa Bay.

The toads proved themselves to be remarkably adaptable, and soon settled in for an easy life in suburbia. Streetlights and lawn lamps provided them with plenty of food by attracting insects; they laid their long strings of thousands of eggs in fish ponds and drainage ditches. (As the name suggests, the Marine Toads are also more tolerant of salt water than most amphibians, and can lay their eggs in brackish estuaries and tide swamps.) The huge paratoid glands on the back of their necks produced a milky white toxin that was powerful enough to kill dogs and protected them from predators — even the eggs are toxic, and kill tadpoles of other frog species that eat them. And unlike most toads, who will only eat live prey that is moving, the Cane Toads learned to eat dry dog food out of the dishes on people's porches, opening up an enormous source of suburban food.

Today, the Cane Toad is one of the most invasive species on the planet. Not only is it thriving in many of the agricultural areas where it was deliberately introduced, but it was also spread by the exotic pet trade. In Australia, it is a major threat to rare native species of marsupial, particularly predators who try to sample the toads and end up getting poisoned. In Bermuda, the Cane Toad is a known threat to the severely endangered Bermuda Skink. In Florida, the invaders are displacing the native Southern Toad, and several thousand dogs and cats are killed each year when they bite the toad or pick it up in their mouths. (Many of our native raccoons and opossums, however, have learned to eat the toads by flipping them onto their backs and eating out their bellies, leaving behind the toxic glands on the toad's back.)

The Cane Toad, meanwhile, is continuing its slow northward invasion. It now reaches as far north as Pasco County, and there appears to be nothing to prevent them from eventually reaching as far as Georgia and perhaps the Carolinas. Within Florida, the Fish and Wildlife Commission has more or less given up on attempting to control the species, though it urges Florida residents to kill the toads wherever they are found.

The Brazilian Pepper

One of our most invasive species is the Brazilian pepper, also known as the Florida holly or sometimes as the Christmas Berry. Introduced as an ornamental, it has now taken over much of the state.

The Brazilian Pepper plant, *Schinus terebinthifolius*, is a large shrub, reaching 15-30 feet in height, with a short trunk, long compound leaves, and large clusters of tiny white flowers that turn into glossy bright red beans in the winter.

Taxonomically, Brazilian Pepper is not really a pepper. It is a member of the Anacardiaceae family, which also includes the cashews, the sumacs, and the poison ivy and poison oaks. Like most of the other plants in its family, Brazilian Pepper produces a protective chemical oil called urushiol, which produces skin irritation and dermatitis on contact. But unlike its relatives Poison Ivy and Poison Oak, Brazilian Pepper's urushiol is found mostly in the sap, and not on the leaves. In its native areas, it is known as the "tame tree" to distinguish it from its more virulent relatives. But if the tree is burned, in a wildfire or as part of a controlled fire, the smoke carries the volatile oils and can cause irritation in anyone nearby.

Because the plant evolved in a harsh environment, it has become tough and adaptable. It can withstand flooding, drought, and forest fires, can grow in either wet or dry soil, and is also able to tolerate high levels of salt and grow in brackish swamps and estuaries. The plant has two separate sexes, with each individual tree having either male or female flowers. Flowering happens in September and October, with clusters of immature green fruit appearing in November and maturing into bright red seed clusters in December. The seeds can remain buried for up to three months and still successfully sprout, and individual trees live about 35 years. The germination rate for the seeds is improved if they travel through the digestive tract of a bird or small mammal (raccoons and opossums eat the seeds). If the trunk is broken off or cut down, it resprouts by sending up new shoots from the roots. The tree grows very rapidly, sometimes as much as ten feet a year.

The Brazilian Pepper's natural range is in Brazil, Paraguay and Argentina. Although it is not actually a pepper plant, the dried fruits are often used in South America as a spice and are sold as "peppercorns".

But it was not because of its peppercorns that the tree has been spread around the world—it is because of its close association with a particular holiday. The dark green leaves and bright red berries resemble Holly, and in tropical areas where Hollies do not grow, it was widely imported for use as Christmas decorations. It was already being grown in Florida as a garden ornamental by the 1840's, where it became known as the "Florida Holly" or the "Christmas Berry". Genetic testing has shown that there were two different sources for Florida's Brazilian Pepper plants—one group came from southeastern Brazil and was imported into the Punta Gorda area around 1925, and the other comes from northern Brazil and was imported into Miami about 1890. Both varieties have now hybridized extensively within Florida. From there, the Brazilian Pepper was sent across the southern US, and quickly escaped cultivation and spread into the wild.

It took about 50 years from the time the plant was widely introduced into the wild until it began aggressively invading and taking over native habitats. It has been speculated that this was the result of adaptations that appeared after hybridization had increased the Brazilian Pepper's gene pool and gave it more genetic diversity.

Once established in a wild area, Brazilian Pepper quickly overwhelms all the local native plants and forms dense monoculture stands, crowding out everything else. It is particularly good at invading areas that have been recently disturbed, such as roadsides, canal banks, urban areas, and places where there have been wildfires. In Florida, over 700,000 acres of habitat have been taken over by this species, where it invades pine flatlands, upland hardwood hammocks, and mangrove marshes.

The species is now considered to be one of the worst invasives in Florida. It is illegal to import or possess the plant, and the state expends considerable effort each year trying to eradicate the invader. These efforts are not very successful. The plant is tough and adaptable and can grow virtually anywhere, limited only by its low tolerance for cold temperatures. Since cut-off trunks will simply resprout, the entire root must be dug out. Only two herbicides have been found effective against Brazilian Pepper — glyphosate and triclopyr. Biologists have investigated over 200 of the tree's natural insect enemies in Brazil to try to find a method of biological control, and two possible insects have been found — a species of sawfly and a thrip — but these have to be thoroughly tested to insure they do not present any danger to any of Florida's native plants.

The Tokay Gecko

One of our invaders is a large unfriendly lizard from southeast Asia with a not-very-polite nickname, that was very popular in the pet trade.

The Geckos are one of the largest groups of lizards, with at least 1500 different species scattered in tropical and temperate areas around the world. Nearly all are nocturnal, sleeping during the day and hunting for insects and smaller animals at night. They are best-known for their complex toe pads which allow them to walk up walls and across ceilings, seemingly defying gravity. The Geckos are also unusual among reptiles in that they communicate vocally, calling to each other in the night using chirps, squeaks or barks.

One of the most familiar of this group of lizards is the Tokay Gecko, *Gekko gecko*, which can be found from southeast Asia down into Indonesia and up into India. (The Bangladesh population is sometimes considered to be a separate subspecies.) This is a large lizard, reaching over a foot long (Tokays are the second-largest species of Gecko in the world), with an attractive color pattern of slate blue or light purple covered with rust-red or orange spots. They have the ability to make their skin patterns lighter or darker, both to blend in with their background and as a method of communication.

Tokays live in rainforest areas, clinging to tree trunks and hunting insects, tree frogs, and smaller lizards at night. The large eyes, with vertical pupils like a cat, give excellent night vision, and like most geckos they have no eyelids—they periodically lick their eyeballs with their tongues to clean them.

The name "tokay" comes from the loud clicking call that the males make during the breeding season, both to attract females and to warn other males away from their territory. During the Vietnam War, American soldiers who heard the geckos calling at night thought that it was Viet Cong guerrillas taunting them with rude English insults from the jungle, and the Tokay Gecko was widely known as the "f*ck you" lizard.

Tokay Geckos reproduce by laying eggs, often in pairs. It is not uncommon for breeding females to lay a pair of eggs every month for four or five months in a row. The eggs have sticky hard shells when laid, and are attached to the underside of a tree branch and guarded by Mom until they hatch. The hatchlings are around 2 inches long. It takes about three years for a young Tokay to reach adulthood. In captivity, they have lived up to 12 years; wild lizards probably live 8-10 years.

What Tokay Geckos are most famous for among reptile-keepers, however, is their sheer belligerence. They may possibly be the meanest lizard you will ever see. They are fiercely territorial and do not tolerate the presence of other Tokay Geckos in their area, or any other intruder—including human keepers. The males, which are larger and brighter than the females, are particularly belligerent. When annoyed, Tokays will puff themselves up with air and gape their jaws at the intruder, and if pressed, they will not hesitate to bite. The jaw muscles are very strong, and an adult Tokay can give a very painful bite that can easily draw blood, and once clamped down on you, it can be hard to get the lizard to let go. Some people have labeled them "the reptilian pit bull". In tropical Asia, where the Tokays are often encouraged or even deliberately released into homes as a way to control cockroaches, spiders and other pests, the humans learn quickly to keep their hands away.

Nevertheless, despite their aggressiveness and their ready willingness to chomp on you, the Tokay Gecko's large size and attractive colors made it enormously popular in the exotic pet trade during the 1990's. They were imported from Indonesia and the Philippines by the thousands, often selling in pet shops for ten dollars or less.

Although pet Tokays are tough and easy to care for as well as pretty to look at, new and inexperienced reptile keepers soon discovered that the Tokay Gecko is entirely willing to bite the hand that feeds it, and then not let go. Soon, keepers with sore fingers were releasing their now-unwanted pets into the backyard. In the cold northern areas of the US, the lizards quickly died. But in the warmer areas, the tough adaptable Tokays thrived. Today, introduced Tokay Geckos have become established throughout the southern US, particularly Hawaii and Texas. In Florida, small escaped colonies from commercial breeders had been established near Gainesville in the mid-60's, but it wasn't until the reptile pet craze of the 1990's that the state began to be flooded with imports and escapees. Today the lizards are breeding in at least ten Florida counties, including the Keys. They are often found in houses, running across the ceilings at night, and it's not unusual to hear the distinctive gecko call from inside the walls or up in the attic.

For some, the geckos are welcomed, as a means of keeping the house bug-free. Indeed, it was not uncommon for Florida residents to buy a couple Tokays for the specific purpose of releasing them inside to eat cockroaches. But the Tokays also make meals of our Florida tree frogs and smaller lizards, including our smaller native geckos. So far, state wildlife officials consider the introduced Tokays to be a mild threat to native wildlife, but are not making any efforts to eradicate the Tokays, preferring to put their resources into more threatening invaders. The Tokays, once released, tend to stay in the local urban area, preferring to live inside people's houses rather than dispersing out into the surrounding wild countryside, and that limits their spread and prevents them from being a danger to most of Florida's native wildlife. So until the Tokays become more of an actual threat, state wildlife officials, like many Florida residents, are inclined to a "live and let live" policy towards them.

In some areas in their native Asia, Tokay Geckos are eaten as a local delicacy. They are also used in traditional Chinese medicine. They are not yet protected by any conservation treaties, but they are legally protected in some of their native local areas as they have become depleted by the pet trade.

The Walking Catfish

One of our invaders is a seeming impossibility--a fish that breathes air and walks on land.

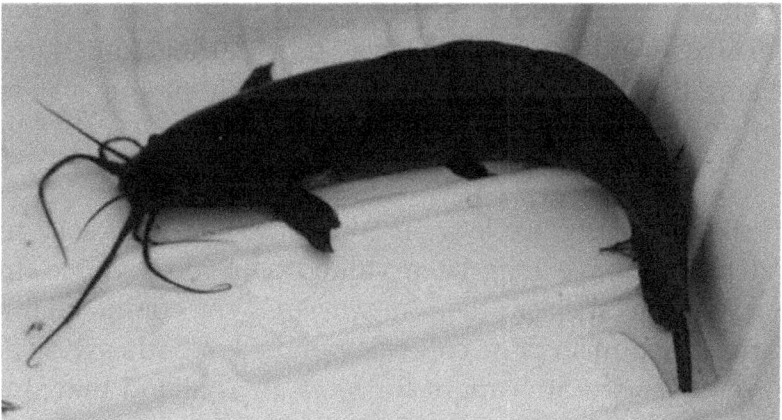

OK, so the Walking Catfish, *Clarias batrachus*, doesn't actually have legs and doesn't really *walk*. But it is pretty good at scrambling across dry ground on its fins, it can gulp air to breathe, and it has invaded Florida.

The Clariid family contains about 100 different species of catfish, organized into 14 different genus names. All of them are freshwater fish, and they can be found in many areas of Africa and southeastern Asia. They are inhabitants of stagnant pools and shallow slow-moving streams, where they dine happily on smaller fish and invertebrate prey as well as aquatic plants and organic matter strained from the bottom muck.

During the dry times of the year the stagnant ponds inhabited by the catfish often dry up and disappear, leaving the fish high and dry. As a result, they have become adapted to moving overland in search of a new pool. By gulping air into a specially-modified pouch in their gill arches, they are able to breathe out of water for as long as their gills stay wet, and by holding themselves up with their muscular pectoral fins and wiggling like a snake, they can travel over land in search of a new home. This has given them the name "Walking Catfish". Their ability to breathe air also allows them to live in warm shallow oxygen-poor water where other fish cannot survive. And in really hard times, they can bury themselves in the mud and aestivate until the waters return. They can go up to four months without food.

Because they are large fish (2-3 feet) and are easy to catch, they have long been valued as a food source. In Africa, the species *Clarias gariepinus* is commercially farm-raised in shallow concrete ponds. In Southeast Asia, several species are caught for food; in Thailand they are called *pla duk nam*, in the Philippines they are known as *hito*, and in Malaysia as *keli*. In Java, the local species is *Clarias batrachus*, known locally as *leleh*.

Although they are not particularly attractive fish, being mostly a dull brown or black color, the Walking Catfish became somewhat popular in the aquarium trade in the 1960's, and a number of species were imported as pets, mostly *C. batrachus* from Thailand and Java. In response, tropical fish breeders in Florida established small breeding colonies to supply the pet industry, and a few people established commercial fish farms to raise the catfish as food. Unfortunately, one of these aqua-farmers, in Palm Beach County, had some escapes when their breeding pond was flooded, and another group of Walking Catfish were liberated when a truck carrying them to Miami was involved in an accident that broke open their shipping container and allowed them to squirm off into the woods. In 1967, after other nations began reporting problems with introduced Walking Catfish invasions, the state of Florida decided to ban the import and possession of the fishes as a precaution— which led to a commercial aquarium breeder in Tampa illegally dumping his adult fish into the nearby Hillsborough River.

In all three areas, the escaped/released fish found Florida to their liking. Within ten years, they had spread to 20 counties in southern Florida, and the three separate established populations had merged into one large group, covering the entire peninsula from Tampa Bay south to the Everglades. The many interconnected ponds and canals in Florida allowed them to spread rapidly, helped along by their ability to walk across roadways and suburban lawns in search of new bodies of water. Today, in some parts of Florida, there are as much as a ton and a half worth of Walking Catfish per acre of wetland.

Initially, it was feared that the voracious invaders would make quick meals out of Florida's many native fish, but for some reason the Florida populations of Walking Catfish seem to be satisfied with the life of a scavenger rather than a predator, and tend to eat mostly detritus and small invertebrates. They also tend to prefer oxygen-poor ephemeral ponds and ditches where other fish are not found. So, fortunately, damage to Florida's native fish species does not appear to be very great. They do seem, however, to have a predilection for farm fish, and Walking Catfish often invade commercial Tilapia farms and make meals out of the inhabitants. Aquaculturalists in south Florida have to put fences around their ponds to keep the invaders out; the catfish cost the Florida fish-farming industry millions of dollars a year in additional expenses and losses.

So far, the temperatures north of Tampa Bay seem to be too low for the fish to tolerate, and their spread seems to have halted. The Walking Catfish are also found in some other states where they have escaped or been dumped, including California, Arizona, Georgia, Connecticut and Massachusetts, but they are not reported to be breeding there. (The Federal Government has now banned Walking Catfish everywhere in the US.) In Florida they breed at one year of age, at a length of around 12 inches, the males making nests from vegetation in shallow water and guarding the eggs and newly-hatched young. In their native Southeast Asia *C batrachus* can get up to two feet in length, but in Florida they rarely exceed 12-14 inches.

The introduced catfish have become a favorite prey for many of Florida's egrets and herons. Large numbers of the nocturnal fish are also squashed while trying to cross roads, particularly during mass movements from pond to pond on rainy nights. In some areas, immigrant populations from Asia catch the catfish for food.

Although the Walking Catfish has not done as much damage to Florida aquatic life as was first feared, it is still considered an undesirable invader. But because it is tough and adaptable, state officials have pretty much accepted the fact that the "fish that walks" is probably now a permanent resident.

The Spectacled Caiman

Florida's most famous resident is the American Alligator. But the state is also home to one of the Alligator's much smaller cousins – which is not supposed to be here.

In the late 1940's and early 1950's, Florida was undergoing a tourist boom, as post-war middle-class Americans with disposable income sought vacations in the land of sun and sand. And one of the most popular "souvenirs" that tourists brought home with them were baby American Alligators. Since baby gators don't remain "babies", most of the ones that survived the often-improper care they received were set loose outside somewhere (or, as legend has it, were flushed down the toilet to populate the underground sewer tunnels).

By 1960, legal steps were taken, at both the state and federal level, to first regulate and then to completely ban the trade in baby Alligators. So, the pet industry made a substitution—dealers began importing juvenile Spectacled Caimans (*Caiman crocodilus*) from Central America. These were often sold as "Alligators" or "Dwarf Alligators", and most of the people who purchased them probably never knew the difference. By 1970, tens of thousands of baby caimans had entered the US. Most of them, like the baby Alligators before, quickly died.

The few who survived soon got too big and too hard to handle, and were often dumped by their owner. In most places, these quickly died too: Caimans are very susceptible to cold and cannot tolerate winter temperatures in the US. The sole exception to this was South Florida, where the climate suited them. By 1968, Spectacled Caiman nests were being found in Dade County, confirming that a breeding population had already been established. By 1974, there were enough Caimans in Florida to alarm state wildlife officials, who introduced a program to exterminate them from the area around Homestead Air Force Base. That effort failed, and the Caiman continued to spread. They got a boost in 1992, when Hurricane Andrew destroyed a number of exotic-pet breeding facilities and released a number of species, including Spectacled Caiman, into the wild.

Today, there are breeding populations in Dade and Broward Counties, and non-breeding groups have been sighted as far north as Palm Beach and Seminole Counties. In addition, breeding colonies have become established in Puerto Rico and in Cuba (where the Caiman is a competitor with the endangered Cuban Crocodile). Individual escapees have been reported all over the US, but only southern Florida provides a climate in which they can survive the winter.

The Spectacled Caiman is one of the smaller crocodilian species. In its native range, from southern Mexico to northern Argentina, it can reach a length of eight feet; in Florida it does not seem to get any bigger than five or six feet. The name comes from a curved ridge of bone across the face just in front of the eyes, which make it look as if it is wearing glasses.

Although it is shy and not aggressive towards humans, the Spectacled Caiman will readily defend itself if it is cornered. It is an opportunistic feeder, taking anything from aquatic birds to fish to large insects. The state of Florida considers it a potential threat to waterbirds, and also a potential competitor for space with the Alligator and the endangered American Crocodile (though ecologically the Caiman prefers fresh water while the Crocodile inhabits brackish areas). In addition, the Spectacled Caiman is a carrier of tongue-worms which can parasitize native fish species.

In areas where they can breed, the females will construct nests on shore from rotting vegetation, and lay up to 30-35 hard-shelled eggs inside. As these incubate, the mother will guard the nest from predators, and then helps dig out the babies once they hatch. The young Caimans will stay with their mother for several months until they are big enough to go off on their own. It's not unusual for an adult female to stand watch over a large group of youngsters from several different mothers. Baby Caimans are eaten by Florida's egrets and herons, as well as by large turtles and raccoons. As with other crocodilians, the sex of the hatchling is determined by the temperature at which it incubates: cooler temperatures produce males, and warmer temperatures produce females. The hatchlings are bright yellow and black, but fade to a greenish grey as they get older. They reach maturity in about four years.

Because most of their skin is studded with bony plates, Spectacled Caimans are not valued very much for their leather. Like all crocodilians, however, they are legally protected and their international trade is regulated. In most areas of South and Central America, Spectacled Caimans are not considered to be seriously endangered, though the Colombian populations are threatened.

Since Caimans are so sensitive to weather, they have so far been limited to the extreme south of Florida and do not appear to be expanding their range. As a result, state wildlife officials have given it a low priority, especially since the attempt to eliminate the species in the Homestead area was unsuccessful. As long as they stay at a low density and do not appear to be harming the native American Crocodile populations, Florida seems content to just allow Mother Nature to keep the Caimans fenced in.

The Tilapia

For most people, the only Tilapia fish they see is on the dinner menu: they are popular in seafood restaurants. But the Tilapia has also become a familiar sight in Florida, easily recognized by the large saucer-shaped nests that it digs out in warm shallow waters.

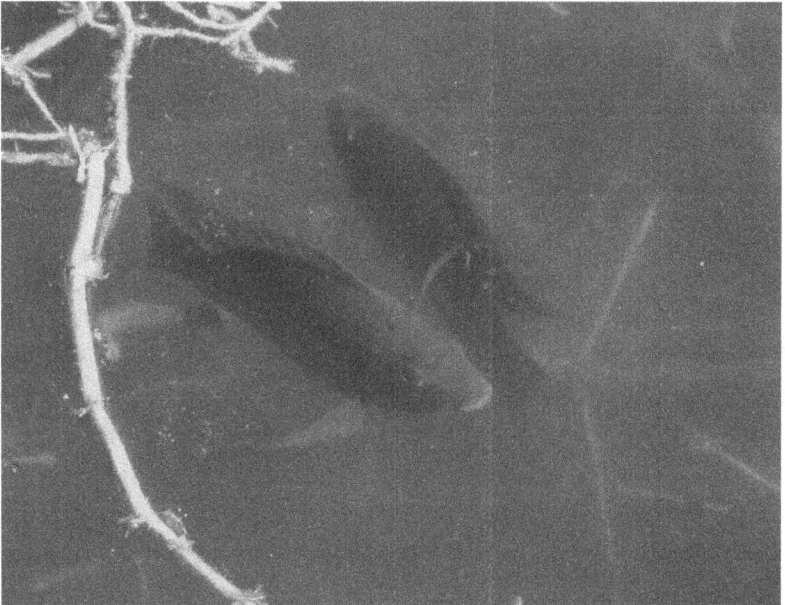

There are over 100 species in the Tilapia group, found virtually throughout Africa. In appearance, they look something like an American sunfish, about a foot long with thick protrusible lips.

They are an important food source for people who live near their lake habitats. (The name comes from "*thiape*", the local South African native word for "fish".) Since there are several species of Tilapia in the Sea of Galilee, they are sometimes known as "St Peter's Fish". The ancient Egyptians raised Tilapia for food in artificial ponds, a practice later copied by the Romans. Today, Tilapia are widely raised in captivity, in outdoors ponds or indoors tanks, and are heavily exported as food. They have been called "aquatic chickens".

In the 1960's, "aquaculture" was widely embraced as a sustainable method of providing high-quality protein food to people in poverty-stricken areas with few resources. And Tilapia, which eat a varied diet of aquatic plants, algae, and invertebrates, were the fish of choice for these artificial fish farms. As a result, the fish were exported to virtually every tropical area on earth. By the 1970's, it was realized what a mistake this was, as escaped or accidentally-released Tilapia established themselves in dozens of countries from Australia to South America, and became threats to native species. They are now listed as one of the "100 Most Invasive Species".

Although Tilapia are tropical fish and cannot tolerate cool temperatures, they found parts of the southern United States to their liking, including Florida. The fish took several different pathways to get here: some were introduced as farmed food-fish, some were deliberately stocked by state officials as a potential game fish, some were brought in to help control invasive aquatic plants, and some were imported by local electric companies to inhabit wastewater ponds where the water temperature was too high for native fish to survive. Finally, they were sometimes introduced as a method of mosquito control, since they eat larvae. The first established wild populations seem to have been found in Hillsborough County in 1971. These were likely escapees from a series of water-filled phosphate pits, where Tilapia had been introduced ten years earlier to control the overgrowth of Duckweed.

Today, there are several different species of Tilapia established in the US, including the Spotted Tilapia, the Blue Tilapia, the Nile Tilapia, the Redbelly Tilapia, and the Mozambique Tilapia. These freely interbreed and hybridize. For the most part, the Blue Tilapia is the most cold-tolerant, and the Spotted Tilapia the least. The Blue Tilapia (*Oreochromis aureus*) is the most widespread, found throughout Florida and across the southern US, sometimes extending as far north as Pennsylvania. The Spotted Tilapia (*Tilapia mariae*) is more limited to southern Florida. Since it has some tolerance for saltwater, it is sometimes found in shallow estuaries along seashores.

The Blue Tilapia is most conspicuous during the spring breeding season, when the males excavate a large shallow dish-shaped depression in the mud along shallow lake shores. Although these bowl-nests are crowded close together, each male viciously defends his nest against all the others. After attracting a female, the pair will mate and produce thousands of eggs—but these are not laid in the male's nest. Instead, the female takes the fertilized eggs into her mouth and swims away. In a strategy known as "mouth-brooding", she will protect the eggs in her mouth until they hatch, with the tiny baby fishes also dashing into Mommy's mouth whenever they need protection. After about a month, the young fish are big enough to wander off on their own.

In a misguided effort to control the smaller Spotted Tilapia in southern Florida, officials introduced the non-native Peacock Cichlid to eat the young Tilapia. But the Tilapia proved able to adapt, and now there are two introduced species where there was just one before. In the rest of Florida, fishermen are encouraged to take as many Tilapia as they can catch (because it is illegal in Florida to possess any live Tilapia, any fish taken by anglers must be immediately killed). They don't put up much of a fight and aren't much of a sport fish, but they are well-known as an excellent panfish. Originally raised as a food source, the Tilapia are a staple item on seafood restaurant menus and in frozen-fish sections at the supermarket. But despite the lack of any legal restrictions on their capture, the fish have proven able to breed far faster than humans can remove them. In many areas where the Tilapia have taken over, they have denuded all the aquatic vegetation and survive only on algae, in conditions where no other fish can survive.

The Melaleuca

Today, Florida spends large amounts of money and resources each year to protect and preserve our wild wetland habitat. One of our most prominent plant invaders, however, was originally introduced to Florida in a deliberate attempt to destroy swamp habitat.

The Melaleuca Tree, is a member of the myrtle family, Latin name Myrtacea. There are about 200 species in the *Melaleuca* genus, found mostly in Australia but also extending into Malaysia and some of the Solomon Islands.

The species that concerns us is *Melaleuca quinquenervia*. In its native Australia, it is known as the paperbark, the tea tree, or the punk tree. In appearance, it is a smallish tree, about 50-60 feet high, with lance-shaped evergreen leaves, bottle-brush clusters of flowers, and its most prominent feature—a light-colored bark that peels extensively from the trunk, making it look something like an American birch tree. The leaves contain camphor and smell like medicine when crushed. (The oil from a closely related tree, *M. alternifolia*, is commercially extracted and used as an antibiotic and fungicide.)

In its native Australia, the Melaleuca grows along waterways and marshes. It produces an immense quantity of fruits and seeds, which make it a valuable food source for birds and fruit-eating bats. It is often intentionally planted as a nectar source for beehives, and is also widely used as an ornamental tree or windbreak. Because Melaleuca uses large quantities of water, it is not commonly found in the large dry Outback areas. In some parts of Australia the tree is being threatened by loss of its habitat through development, and conservation measures are being taken to protect it.

In the early 1900s, sugar and citrus growers in Florida were searching for an effective way to drain the state's marshes and wetlands to produce new farmland. One idea was to plant lots of Melaleuca trees, which would then take up large amounts of water through their roots and respire it away through their leaves, helping to dry up the swamps. By 1910 the Australian trees were a common sight in South Florida. In the 1930's Melaleuca seeds were intentionally dropped into the Everglades by airplane, in an attempt to dry out and reclaim the "useless swamp". Because they grew so rapidly, they were also planted in parks and backyards as ornamentals, along canals and ponds as support props for banks, and some were commercially grown for their wood.

It turned out to be a disaster. With no natural checks on their growth, the trees exploded, quickly invading nearly the whole of south Florida. The oils in the tree's leaves and bark make them flammable, which turned out to be an advantage: when the Melaleucas were ignited by Florida's yearly lightning-triggered grassfires, it triggered them to immediately drop their large number of seeds. This allowed the trees to beat the native plants to the freshly-cleared ground, and their rapid growth rate—as much as 6 feet a year—then enabled the Melaleucas to dominate and form extensive stands of monoculture. Experiments have shown that a one square mile area can be 95% dominated by Melaleuca in just 25 years. Today, Melaleuca covers an estimated half-million acres of area, particularly in the endangered Everglades habitat.

Fortunately, as a tropical tree, the potential range for the plant is limited. Although the adult trees can tolerate a degree of freezing, the young seedlings cannot. As a result, the invader is only rarely found north of Tampa Bay, and is mostly concentrated in the six frost-free counties near Miami and the Keys. Melaleuca can, however, tolerate brackish water and often invades mangrove swamps.

The damage has been extensive. The Melaleucas crowd out and displace native trees, and by dominating fire-cleared areas, they prevent the normal process of succession. Although the trees produce large quantities of seed and fruit, most native Florida birds and mammals don't eat them (though honeybees seem to like the flowers as a nectar source). And, as originally intended, the Melaleucas remove large amounts of water, reducing critically-endangered wetlands habitat. The tree is listed as one of the "100 Most Invasive Species", and is considered a serious danger to Florida's native ecosystems.

Efforts to eradicate the invader have so far not been very successful. If the tree is cut or damaged, it induces a mass seedfall, which leads to more trees later. Melaleuca is also resistant to most herbicides.

Because the wood is rot-resistant as well as fungus and termite repellant, the state of Florida has been encouraging the commercial harvesting and grinding of Melaleuca stands as a source of landscaping mulch and wood chips (and as a means of destroying the trees). In 1995, Florida also began releasing an imported Australian weevil (*Oxyops vitiosa*), which attacks the tree's seeds, as a method of biological control. But so far these control methods have not been very effective.

The Fire Ant

If you've ever spent some time outside in Florida, then you've probably met the Fire Ant. The numerous sandy mounds, often several to a colony, are a familiar site in rural fields and urban lawns, and encounters often end with a painful raised welt that lasts for several days. The Fire Ant may be our most unwelcome invader of all.

There are about 280 species of fire ant, all in the genus *Solenopsis*. They can be found in virtually every tropical and subtropical area on earth, and get their name from their ability to deliver painful stings when disturbed. Biologically, "ants" are wasps that have shed their wings and taken to living underground. Many ant species, including the *Solenopsis*, have retained the stinging apparatus of their wasp ancestors. The stings can deliver a venom, made mostly of alkaloids, that varies in potency from species to species.

In Florida, our native species of fire ant is *Solenopsis geminata*. These live in underground colonies excavated in the sandy soil, marked on the surface by a mound of dirt. Inside this mound are chambers where, on clear days, the larvae and pupae are brought to warm themselves in the sun-heated sand. If you disturb the mound, you will see the worker ants frantically carrying the young back into the subterranean nest. *S geminata* is capable of stinging, but their venom is not all that potent, and they prefer to defend the nest with a special caste of soldiers — individual ants with disproportionately large heads and strong jaws, who attack intruders by biting. Native Florida fire ants are not much bother to people.

Sometime in the 1930's, however, a new species arrived in Florida, probably by stowing away in a cargo shipment. The Red Fire Ant, *Solenopsis invicta*, is native to the Amazon forests of Brazil. (The Latin name *"invicta"* means "unbeatable", which may turn out to be sadly prophetic.) It was originally believed to be just a color morph of the Black Fire Ant (*S. saevissima richteri*), but subsequent study has shown it to be a separate species. (The Black Fire Ant is also an invader in the US, but so far its range is limited to parts of Alabama and Mississippi.)

Like our native fire ants, the Red Fire Ant lives in a large underground colony with tens of thousands of individuals. After a new queen has mated, she will land in a suitable spot, tear off her wings, and dig out a nesting chamber. The first batch of workers are very small (called "minims")--they live just long enough to help raise a couple generations of new workers. The vast majority of nests have only one reproductive queen, and all the worker ants are her daughters. For reasons that are not well-understood, however, a certain small percentage of Fire Ant colonies will have more than one queen, sometimes several dozen, sharing a single colony. These queens can be entirely unrelated—apparently, some solitary queens are able to move into an existing colony and set up housekeeping, with the existing ants accepting the new queen and her new daughters as members of the group.

The workers come in three different sizes. The "minors" are the ones who tend the young and maintain the nest. The "media" are larger in size, and do most of the foraging for food. The "majors" are the biggest, and they play the role of "soldiers", defending the nest from intruders. When the mound is disturbed (such as when a human inadvertently stands or sits on one) the soldiers will emerge from their underground chambers, stealthily climb onto the intruder, then, at a chemical signal, they will all sting at once. Latching onto the intruder's skin with their jaws, they will plunge the stinger at the end of their abdomen into the enemy and release their venom. Since the intruder gets no warning, it may be suddenly stung by dozens or even hundreds of ants. In small animals like mice or lizards, this often brings death. In humans, each sting will produce a swelling as the necrotoxic venom eats away a small bit of flesh, usually resulting in a distinctive white pustule the next day, which will then burn and itch painfully for several days afterwards. In some cases, such as incapacitated patients in nursing homes or small toddlers, such attacks have been fatal. A number of people are also allergic to the venom, like bee stings, and even a single sting can cause a lethal case of anaphylactic shock.

As a "superorganism" containing thousands or tens of thousands of individuals, Fire Ant colonies are also efficient hunters, scouring the areas around the nest for anything edible. They will attack and eat animal prey such as ground-dwelling birds, lizards, toads and rodents. This has made them a conservation threat to a number of Florida species, who have no previous evolutionary experience with the ants and therefore have no effective defense against them. And although the ants only rarely eat seeds or young plant shoots, their hard earthen nest mounds are a hazard to agricultural machinery and can cause significant damage.

It is not known exactly when or where *Solenopsis invicta* first entered the US. It is known that Black Fire Ants, *S. saevissima richteri*, became established around Mobile AL in 1918, likely from a shipment originating in Brazil. Sometime in the late 1920's or early 1930's, the closely-related Red Fire Ant followed, being first detected in the Florida Panhandle. It may have entered either in Pensacola FL or Mobile AL. By 1945 the species was firmly established, and began a slow but steady expansion. Today, the Red Fire Ant is found throughout the entire Southeast and into Texas, with colonies found locally all the way to California and up into Virginia and Maryland. The tropical ants cannot tolerate freezing conditions, so it is likely that climate conditions will prevent them from reaching much further. They have also become established in the Caribbean, Australia, and Southeast Asia. In Florida, they can be found in every county.

The Florida folk remedy to dispose of Fire Ants is to pour boiling water down the mound to kill them. Since the underground colonies are quite large, this can take as much as three or four gallons of water. Commercial fire ant treatments consist of insecticides contained inside granules of corn powder. These are scattered on the mounds, where the workers carry them into the nest and feed them to the others. Both of these methods will fail, however, unless the queen is killed, and this can be a particular challenge in multi-queen colonies. Some states, including Florida, have also been attempting biological warfare against the ants, by releasing a species of *Pseudacteon* fly known as the "brain-eating fly" which parasitizes the ants and kills the colony. A type of protozoan parasite and a fungus which attacks the ants is also under investigation as a possible biological control.

There are some indications that the Florida population of colonies has been decreasing in recent years, though this may be just a temporary response to weather conditions. So far, it seems that *S invicta* is indeed "unbeatable".

The Asian Carp

Sometimes called the "Giant Flying Goldfish", the Asian Carp is best known for its spectacular leaps out of the water when frightened, making them a serious danger to boaters.

Carp are, biologically, just giant minnows. Belonging to the Cyprinid family of fishes, they are widely distributed around the world. Their best-known member is *Carassius auratus*, the plain ole ordinary petshop Goldfish, which is native to eastern Asia, and its close relative *Carassius carpio*, the Koi, also known in the wild as the Common Carp. Other Asian carp species include the Grass Carp (*Ctenopharyngodon idella*) and the Silver Carp (*Hypophthalmichthys molitrix*).

In their native areas, the Asian carp species are widely-used as food fish (though they have a lot of bones, and wild ones have a reputation for a "muddy" taste). In particular, the Silver Carp is widely used in aquaculture, and has been imported to at least 88 different countries to be raised as a food fish. So it was probably inevitable that escapees would become established. Although the wild population in China is now considered a threatened species, captive and introduced Silver Carp are common all over the world. They prefer quiet stagnant water, where they can tolerate low oxygen levels that would kill most other fish.

Asian Carp species, including both Silver and Grass Carp, were imported into the United States in the 1960's. Escapees in Arkansas established themselves in the Mississippi River after a flood, and spread outwards. Since the fish can reproduce quickly and eat a lot, they can out-compete native fishes and crowd them out. By the 1990's, Asian Carp had been established in 23 states. Federal and state wildlife officials, realizing the tremendous ecological damage that would happen if the invasives reached the Great Lakes, constructed a series of electric "fish fences" to keep them out.

In Florida, the Grass Carp was introduced intentionally. While the Silver Carp is a filter feeder that makes its living by straining phytoplankton from the water, Grass Carp eat aquatic plants. So, back in the 1990's, Florida wildlife officials decided to utilize the species as a biological weapon against the many varieties of invasive non-native water plants (including Water Lettuce, Hydrilla, and Water Hyacinth) that have become ecological threats in the state. To insure that the Carp themselves would not become just another invasive species, fish eggs are chemically treated to form a "triploid" breed, with three copies of each chromosome instead of the normal two. This makes the fish sterile and incapable of breeding. The sterile Carp were introduced into lakes and rivers all over Florida. (The fish will still mate and spawn as usual, but the resulting eggs are infertile and don't hatch.) Since the Carp were intentionally released by the state as a biological control on invasive plants, it is illegal to catch or harm them.

So, why do the Giant Flying Goldfish try to kill boaters and kayakers?

Well, they are just trying to protect themselves. In the wild, the fish are prey for a number of predators, and their natural defense, when they are startled by something, is to leap wildly out of the water to escape the threat. Although Asian carp species can reach three feet in length and weigh over 50 pounds, their powerful muscles can push them as much as ten feet out of the water. And since the fish tend to hang around in schools, when a group of them is scared by a boater or kayaker, there may be several dozen of them leaping in all random directions. It is a veritable barrage of fish.

It's a serious matter. Even a 1-2 foot Carp is big enough to cause some intense damage if it hits a boater or swimmer. There have been instances of people receiving broken jaws or ribs from flying Carp impacts, and one reported death.

Fortunately, Florida officials tightly control the number of Carp that they release. And so far there are no populations of viable invasive Carp species that have made their way to Florida. At least not yet.

The Cuban Tree Frog

The Cuban Tree Frog is the largest tree frog in North America. And with an appetite to match, it has become a serious threat to native Florida wildlife.

The Cuban Tree Frog, *Osteopilus septentrionalis*, is a member of the large Hylid tree frog family which contains dozens of members, but it has a number of anatomic specialties that place it apart, and it is classed in a genus of its own. The skin is rough and warty, and one oddity is that the skin on the top of the head is firmly attached to the roof of the skull. Like other tree frogs, the Cuban is arboreal and spends all its time off the ground. It uses the large sticky pads on the ends of its toes to climb around on tree branches, rock faces, or the sides of buildings. Occasionally, the frogs will seek a daytime shelter inside an electrical circuit box, and end up frying themselves and shorting out the power.

To prevent itself from drying out, the frog's skin is coated with a thin waxy layer that holds in moisture. When threatened, the Cuban Tree Frog can also produce a slimy mucus on its skin that is an irritant to the eyes and mouth of potential predators. Unlike the more familiar pond frogs, tree frogs are not very good swimmers and never enter water except to lay eggs.

During the tropical rainy season, the males develop a dark patch of rough skin on their thumbs (which helps them hold on to females for mating) and will congregate around any semi-permanent body of water that does not contain any fish to eat the eggs—drainage ditches, retention ponds, even swimming pools. The mating call, which is particularly enthusiastic after a rainstorm, is a grating trill that sounds sort of like a rusty gate. The females can lay as many as 1,000 eggs at a time, stuck together in a floating jellylike mass, which usually hatch in just a day or two. The tadpoles feed mostly on algae, but have been known to kill and eat tadpoles of other frog species. Depending on the water temperature, they can hatch and develop into froglets in as little as four weeks. The developed froglets are about half an inch long when they hop off into the trees. They can live as long as ten years in captivity, though wild frogs probably die long before that.

The Tree Frog is found naturally in Cuba, the Cayman Islands and the Bahamas, where it sleeps during the day (usually pressed up against a tree branch to be inconspicuous) and becomes active at night, hunting insects, smaller frogs, and other prey. The females are generally bigger than the males, and can reach a body length of 5.5 inches. Cuban Tree Frogs are usually a drab greenish grey color, but they can control the pigment cells in their skin and are able to change color, usually becoming dark brown or purplish in cooler conditions and light grey when warm. Most often there are darker bands on the rear legs, and the underside of the legs and belly has bright yellow patches. The eyes are very large, with lovely gold flecks in the iris.

Despite their large size, Cuban Tree Frogs can stay pretty inconspicuous. Because of this, they are often unintentionally carried around from place to place, stuck to the side of a packing crate or onto the stem of a potted plant. They have therefore hitchhiked their way around the world, becoming established throughout the Caribbean islands and other tropical areas like Hawaii. The frogs are also prominent in the pet trade, and escaped/released pets have added to their dispersal.

Reports of Cuban Tree Frogs in Florida go back to the 1920s in Miami, where they probably arrived as stowaways in cargo containers. The species was definitively established in South Florida by 1950, long before the pet trade began to import them by the thousands. Almost certainly they had been floating across the Caribbean to the mainland after storms and hurricanes, on floating vegetation mats and uprooted trees, for millennia, but were apparently never able to establish themselves. But once human cities appeared, the Cuban Tree Frogs found that habitat to their liking—

there are fewer predators, lots of suitable prey, and urban areas are even a little warmer than their surroundings. Despite the fact that a variety of Florida predators, from racer snakes to raccoons, will eat them, the Cubans are apparently able to reproduce enough to keep expanding their population. The frogs are able to thrive in close contact with the humans, and have steadily spread north to the Jacksonville area. Since they cannot tolerate freezing conditions (the unusually cold Florida winters of 2010 and 2011 temporarily wiped many of the invaders out), that may be the limit of their expansion.

The frogs are harmless to humans (aside from the irritation sometimes caused by their skin secretions). But they are not so harmless to native Florida wildlife. Cuban Tree Frogs are big, perpetually hungry, and will eat anything that moves which they can fit in their mouths. The biggest impact seems to be on our native tree frog species, who are not only crowded out of habitat and breeding areas by the invaders, but are often swallowed whole as a Tree Frog lunch. While acknowledging that the Cuban Tree Frog is now probably a permanent resident, the State of Florida nevertheless encourages people to kill the frogs wherever they are found, by sealing them inside a plastic baggie and putting them in the freezer overnight.

The Rhesus Monkey

In the early years of Florida tourism, many entrepreneurial showmen took advantage of the state's tropical climate to set up staged "jungle" attractions. And thanks to them, Florida has one of its most adaptable and intelligent invasive species.

There are dozens of monkey species inhabiting South and Central America, but the US is (other than humans) completely primate-less. Or at least it was until the 1930's. That's when the Rhesus Monkey was introduced to Florida.

According to local legend, the monkeys were brought here in 1939, when Hollywood came to Silver Springs, just north of Tampa Bay, to film one of its popular "Tarzan" movies with Johnny Weissmuller, titled "Tarzan Finds a Son". As background, it is said, the filmmakers packed along some Rhesus Monkeys—which promptly ran off into the trees and were never found.

Alas, that story is a myth. There were no monkeys of that species used in the filming. Instead, the most likely origin story for the Florida Rhesus troop is that, in 1938, a local promoter who called himself "Colonel" Tooney set up a "jungle boat ride" attraction, and imported three pairs of Rhesus Monkeys for the tourists to look at. Within days they had escaped their island and were running free, and while Colonel Tooney was unable to recapture them, he was able to feed them regularly with fruits and monkey chow to keep them near the riverbank where the tourists could see them. Over time, the monkeys did what monkeys do, the troop got bigger, and split into first two, then three separate groups. By the 1980s, there were three populations, each with a number of troops. Around 300 Rhesus were living in two locations near the original Silver Springs release site, while another 250 or so had moved to the nearby Ocala National Forest.

For the most part, the primate invaders have been pretty harmless. They seem to do no damage to Florida's native species, though the monkeys may on occasion frighten off human residents as they raid backyard gardens and fruit trees. Some of the locals feed the monkeys in the wintertime. The local Alligators have also learned to leap out of the water and nab the primates off overhanging tree branches.

In 1984, though, Florida wildlife officials decided to wage an all-out effort to remove the invaders. In all, 217 of the Rhesus were trapped and sold to zoos or research labs. But it was quickly realized that the monkeys were clever and canny, and although wildlife officials have captured some 700 individuals in the past ten years, nobody thinks it makes any serious dent in the primate population. The most apparent problem seems to be that many of the captured Rhesus were found to be infected with the herpes-B virus, and could present a potential danger if they were to bite a human or a pet. The FWC now warns people to stay away from the primates.

Today, the original three pairs of Monkeys have expanded to an estimated 1000 individuals, and Rhesus sightings have been reported from as far as Jacksonville, 100 miles away. But the most celebrated Rhesus sighting was in 2008, 100 miles in the other direction in St Petersburg, when several residents reported seeing a "Mystery Monkey" in their yards. Photos ID'd it as a Rhesus, and most people assumed that it was a wanderer from the Silver Springs colony (though, as a solitary individual, it may also have been an illegal pet that escaped or was released). For the next four years, the Wildlife Commission tried to capture the Rhesus, who evaded all attempts. "Mystery Monkey" became a media celebrity, and got his own Facebook page and Twitter account as local and national newspapers followed his adventures. Finally, in 2012, the Rhesus was successfully darted and tranquilized. He now lives in a zoo in nearby Pasco County.

Although the Rhesus troops are the most successful primates known to be breeding in the Florida wild, other species also turn up from time to time. Back in the 50's, a group of Vervet Monkeys escaped from a roadside zoo near Ft Lauderdale and headed for the trees, where their descendents can still be found on the grounds of the local airport. In 2008, another group of 15 Patas Monkeys escaped a private zoo north of Tampa: state officials were able to trap 14 of them, and the last one was shot by a hunter.

The Kudzu

The Kudzu may well be the most famous invasive plant species in the world. It has been celebrated and condemned in poetry and in folk music, and has been notably referred to as "the vine that ate the South".

In 1876, as part of its 100ᵗʰ birthday celebration, the US sponsored a Centennial Exposition in Philadelphia. Countries from around the world were invited to participate and set up pavilions to show off their national culture and heritage. In the pavilion set up by Japan, hostesses handed out a lovely little potted vine related to the peas, native to Japan and China, with sweet fragrant flowers and attractive leaves. It was the Kudzu, *Pueraria lobata*.

Two of the Centennial's visitors were Lillie and Charles Pleas, who owned the Glen Arden Nursery in Chipley FL. Enchanted with the attractive little plant, they took a few back to Florida with them. The Kudzu vines found the Florida climate to their liking. In their native Asia, cold temperatures killed the vines back to the rootstock each winter, which limited their growth. But in subtropical Florida they were warm all year round, and grew freely. The vine formed an immense taproot, half a foot wide, several feet deep, and weighing as much as 400 pounds, which then sent out as many as three dozen runners from each root crown. Expanding as much as a foot a day during good summer weather (some legends assert that you can *hear* a stand of Kudzu vines growing) the runners reached out to cover everything around them. When the stem nodes touched the ground they took root, often then breaking off and forming a new plant. The Glen Arden Nursery began selling them by mail order as garden vines. They became particularly popular in many places as quick-growing shade plants for outside porches and garden trellises.

By the 1920's, the vine had also been discovered by livestock keepers. Goats, sheep, and cattle seemed to like the plant, it was high in protein and nutrients, and it grew stupendously fast. It seemed like a winner, and Kudzu was now planted in pastures all across the southeastern US. The constant grazing helped keep it under control.

Things really started going wrong in the 1930's. The Civilian Conservation Corps was formed to provide jobs for people during the Great Depression by carrying out conservation work outdoors. One of its many projects was erosion control, and thousands of people were put to work for the Soil Conservation Service planting ground cover on bare hillsides to prevent wind and rain from washing the soil away. The plant of choice in the South was Kudzu. From Florida to Texas, farm hillsides and patches of bare dirt were systematically covered with Kudzu vines. "Kudzu Clubs" were formed to promote and advertise the "miracle vine", and the Federal Government went so far as to pay farmers $8 for each acre they planted with Kudzu. It was also used to line bare road banks. In all, the Soil Conservation Service planted 3 million acres with 85 million Kudzu cuttings.

But as the Great Depression dragged on, many farmers found themselves unable to make a living, and in desperation they sold (or simply deserted) their land and moved to the city hoping to find work. For the Kudzu vines, left behind and abandoned in their fields, it was the opportunity of a lifetime. With no natural enemies and now no farmers or grazing animals to keep them in check, they exploded.

Although the US Department of Agriculture continued to promote the use of Kudzu vines as ground cover through the 1940's, by 1953 they realized they had unleashed a monster. Throughout the South, the fast-growing vines were now covering over a million acres of rural area and had also invaded urban roadsides and parks. Like a green tidal wave, the dense leaves completely overgrew and covered buildings, fences, road signs, trees, telephone poles, electric lines, and anything else that would hold still long enough, shading out every native plant under it and often forming a solid unbroken wall of Kudzu. The USDA removed the plant from its recommended list of ground covers, but the damage had already been done. By 1972 the Kudzu infestation had more than doubled, and the Federal Government outlawed its possession. By 2015, the creeping Kudzu was still expanding at around 150,000 acres per year. In Florida as in other states, Kudzu is listed as a Category 1 Noxious Weed.

The search now turned to a way to get rid of it. Unfortunately, Kudzu is resistant to most of the common herbicides, and killing the plants completely requires multiple doses over a period of several years. A number of the plant's natural enemies from China have been investigated for use as possible biological weapons, including sawflies, beetles and weevils, but nearly all of them turned out to also attack commercially important plants like soybeans. Some farmers have turned to a low-tech solution: a herd of goats or cattle can eat the plants faster than they can grow, but it still takes several years to eradicate it completely. The vine can also be laboriously dug up by hand and burned, but that costs around $2,000 per acre—and since even a single length of runner left behind can root itself and start growing again, it often fails. There seemed to be no good way to eradicate Kudzu once it was established. So perhaps the vine would eat the entire South after all.

But the story continues......

Sometime around 2009, a species of stink bug from Asia apparently hitchhiked its way to the US aboard an airplane, establishing itself near the Atlanta Airport and spreading out from there, reaching northern Florida in 2011. It is called the Kudzu Bug, and it lives by sucking the sap from Kudzu plants. In some areas, it has now reduced the amount of Kudzu by almost two-thirds.

But sadly, this unplanned biological weapon also has a side effect—it likes to feast on commercial soybeans as well. So now the Kudzu Bug is well on its way to establishing itself as yet another harmful invader.

The Capybara

People who wander around in the wilds of northern Florida may be shocked to encounter a "rodent of unusual size" that looks like an enormous guinea pig. This is the Capybara, a giant South American rodent that has now made Florida its home.

The largest group of living mammals are, by far, the rodents, with about 1500 species. And the largest of the living rodents is the Capybara, *Hydrochoerus hydrochaeris*. Weighing in at around 100 pounds, one of the Capybara's closest living relatives are the familiar petshop Guinea Pigs or Cavies. Like the Guinea Pig, the Capybara is native to South America, but unlike its tiny mountain-dwelling cousin, the Capybara is an animal of riverbanks and canals.

Capybaras once lived in North America. During the Ice Ages, there were two different species of Capybara living in the southern US, including Florida. They went extinct about 10,000 years ago—likely with a little help from the humans that invaded the area. Since then, Capybaras have been limited to South America.

The scientific name means "water pig", and although it is not actually porcine, the Capybara is definitely a water animal. Ecologically, it is the South American equivalent of the African Hippopotamus. The Capybara has webbed toes to help it swim, and its eyes and nostrils are located at the very top of its face, like an alligator's, allowing it to swim along unnoticed with just its eyes and nose showing. The rodents can also hold their breath for up to five minutes at a time. Although Capybaras happily munch on water plants, their primary food comes from grazing on grasses, tree leaves and fruits along riverbanks, allowing them to retreat into the water if they feel threatened (like Hippos, they usually stay in the water all day and come out to graze at night.)

The females mate only in water, giving birth to an average of four or five young about four months later. Capybaras are highly social animals, living in groups of two dozen or so, with a dominant male and several subordinate males and females, and sometimes congregating in herds of over 100. In the wild, they live for about ten years: their primary predators are Jaguars and Anacondas. Humans also hunted them, and today they are farm-raised in South America for their meat.

In the 1990's, Capybaras became a part of the exotic pet trade in the United States, and a number of them were imported from South America and sold in the US. Although they tame easily and act like huge guinea pigs, becoming socially attached to their keepers, they are big animals and require a lot of space (with their own swimming pool), and inevitably a number of them were released into the wild by keepers who did not want them any longer. Escaped/released Capybaras have been sighted in the wild in California, Louisiana, Ohio, and Texas. There have even been reports of escaped Capybaras in England.

In 1995, a wildlife facility near Gainesville was keeping a group of Capybaras for research when a number of them escaped and vanished into the nearby swamps. Today, the wild Gainesville Capybara colony numbers at least 60 individuals. Elsewhere in Florida, escaped/released pets (kept illegally) often turn up: there have been reports from the Santa Fe, Myakka, and Suwannee Rivers and from the Everglades, and road-killed Capybaras have been confirmed in several places across Florida. In 2001, two young Capybaras managed to escape from the Jacksonville Zoo; one was killed by a car, and during the search for the escapees an unrelated adult female was also found living in the area.

Most of these are likely to be individual escapees or released pets. But Federal wildlife officials have concluded that the Capybaras have established breeding colonies in at least five Florida counties — Alachua, Baker, Bradford, Columbia, and Duval — and have the potential to spread throughout the state.

The Monk Parakeet

The Monk Parakeet, also known as the Quaker Parrot, is colorful, sociable, and highly intelligent, which makes it a popular part of the pet trade. And that is how it came to Florida.

The Monk Parakeet, *Myiopsitta monachus*, is one of the smaller members of the parrot family. Standing about a foot tall, these parrots are a bright electric green with splashes of yellow and blue, and greyish on the chest. They look very similar to the introduced Nanday Parakeet, but lack that bird's distinctive black head. In the wild, they are found in dry areas in Brazil, Bolivia, Uruguay and Argentina. The birds form gregarious flocks that live in large communal nests. Unlike most parrots, which eat mostly seeds, the Monks also eat large amounts of fruit and berries, as well as insects. As the pampas grassland areas in South America were planted with fruit orchards by humans, the birds found perfect habitat and moved in, becoming a serious agricultural pest. In some areas up to 40% of a fruit orchard's yield may be lost to the marauding parrots.

In the 1960s, the Monk Parakeet became enormously popular in the exotic bird trade, prized for its small size, its intelligence, and its skill in learning to talk. By 1968 some 16,000 birds were being taken from the wild and imported to the US each year. By the time the trade in wild birds was restricted, some 65,000 Monk Parakeets had been brought in.

Inevitably, there were escapes; the birds found North America's suburban parks, golf courses, and lawns to their liking, and it wasn't long before feral colonies became established, even in cold northern cities like New York and Chicago (in their native South America they often live in the Andes foothills, and are thus adapted to tolerate colder temperatures than most parrots can stand). In the American south, the Monks are able to make a living from fruit trees and shrubs; in the north, they depend on human birdfeeders to get through the winter.

The USFWS made a brief attempt to eradicate the non-natives and was temporarily successful in removing colonies in California, but it soon became apparent that the effort was futile. Within a few years, Monk Parakeet colonies could be found in New York, Connecticut, Illinois, California, Texas, Louisiana, Oregon, New Jersey, and Alabama. The first nesting colonies were seen in Florida in 1969. Today, there are established populations in over 50 cities, including Tampa, St Petersburg, Jacksonville, Bradenton, Ft Lauderdale, Miami, and Boca Raton. Flocks of the bright green birds can often be seen flying overhead or covering lawns looking for seeds and bugs. The parrots keep in contact with each other through constant screeches and squawks, and flocks can usually be heard from quite a distance away. A number of individuals serve as sentinels, watching out for hawks or other dangers.

So far, the Monk Parakeet's effect on Florida has been minimal. The feral flocks have preferred to stay in the urban areas and have not moved into the rural agricultural regions, where they have the potential to become a serious economic pest. In the cities they do not appear to be having a negative impact on native birds, instead filling the ecological niche that has been empty since its American relative the Carolina Parakeet became extinct. It is estimated that about 35,000 Monk Parakeets now live in Florida.

The bird does have one habit, however, which has made it a serious annoyance to city governments all over Florida. Unlike most parrot species, which nest individually in tree cavities, Monk Parakeets make huge communal nests, woven from twigs and grass stems, which can contain hundreds of birds. These resemble a large section of thatched roof, sometimes ten feet across, and can weigh several hundred pounds. The small number of entrances (usually at the bottom) prevents snakes and other predators from entering, while the thick insulation provides warmth in the winter, and contains a honeycomb of interior chambers for egg-laying. (The Speckled Teal, a kind of duck found in South America, often moves in and makes itself at home in unoccupied chambers inside Monk Parakeet nests.) In the wild, these nests are constructed in tall trees, but in the city, the Monk's favorite spots are urban utility poles.

"Electricity" and "dry twigs" don't go together very well, and it is not unusual for the nests to catch fire, roasting all the birds, destroying the electric lines, and cutting off power to the neighborhood. And during Florida's frequent rainstorms, wet twigs can also short-circuit the power lines, with the same result. And so Florida's electric companies have declared war on the Monk Parakeet. Every so often, the power company will come by and knock down the entire nest. The now-homeless birds will in turn quickly rebuild it. It then becomes a contest of will and endurance, and since the city is prevented from killing the parrots by the potential public outcry from bird-lovers everywhere, the Monks always win. And for many people, the birds, though non-native, are a welcome addition, adding some color and sound to their city life.

The Wild Hog

One of our earliest invasive species in Florida, the wild pig was brought here by the original Spanish settlers in the first decades of the 16th century.

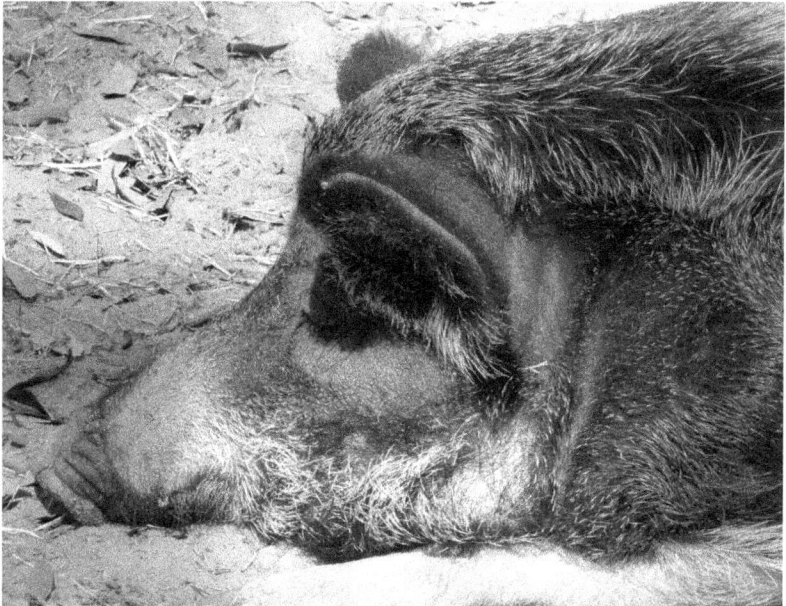

Pigs and humans have a long relationship together. First domesticated thousands of years ago, the pig has accompanied people wherever they have gone. And when Spanish settlers began arriving in the New World after 1492, they brought their hogs along with them. At the time, North America had no pigs at all: the closest thing we had was the Peccary or Javelina, which, though pig-like in appearance and behavior, actually belonged to a different family.

The Javelina lived in the southwest and was not found in Florida, so when Ponce de Leon arrived off the coast in 1521, the pigs that he carried on board his ships were a wondrous sight to the Native Americans—they had never seen such an animal before. By the time Hernan De Soto established a Spanish village near modern-day Naples in 1539, the natives were already keeping hogs as food animals, obtained through trade with sailors and pirates. As Spanish settlements grew in number, so did their pigs. Most often, the animals were left to roam around freely, and were caught and slaughtered as needed. Inevitably, many of them wandered off into the wilderness.

For the next five centuries, natural selection took its course, as the feral pigs spread across the southeast and adapted to their new environment. Wild pigs tend to be a bit smaller than their domestic cousins, but are leaner and lots meaner. Both males (boars) and females (sows) have long sharp tusks that act as effective weapons as well as tools for rooting around in the sand for anything edible. An adult male is usually about five feet long from nose to tail, and around 200 pounds. When European wild boar were introduced to some parts of the US as a game animal in the 1800's, they interbred freely with the local feral hogs, and while Florida never had many European boars, a number of hybrids were brought here for sport hunters. All of our wild pigs, whether feral domestic breeds or European hybrids, are considered to be the single species *Sus scrofa*.

Just like domestic pigs, the wild ferals are prolific breeders, producing two litters of 6 or 7 (sometimes more) piglets each year. They have few predators in Florida, though Panthers, Black Bears and Alligators are known to eat them. Today, there are somewhere around 750,000 feral hogs and hybrids running free, and Florida is exceeded only by Texas in its wild hog population. Although they are found in every Florida county, our wild hogs tend to concentrate in the central part of the state, where there are fewer people and lots of pine-oak forests to provide food and shelter. They also tend to congregate near water: pigs do not have many sweat glands, and their only way of keeping cool in the hot Florida sun is to wallow in mudholes. The males tend to be solitary while the females run in small family groups.

Their favorite food is acorns, but as omnivores wild hogs will feast on anything edible, including tree seedlings, small animals, and agricultural fields or gardens. In many areas they cause serious ecological damage, and wild pigs have been implicated in reducing the numbers of many threatened plant and animal species, including the Longleaf Pine and ground-nesting birds and turtles. Many a suburban gardener has tried unsuccessfully to keep the marauders out—pigs are highly intelligent and can usually find a way through any fence. In addition, wild pigs serve as a reservoir for a number of diseases which can infect livestock.

In an effort to at least prevent the population from spreading further, the state has turned to the "eat them" strategy. Since pigs are already a familiar domestic animal, using them as a food source does not present all the problems with palatability and acceptance that other wild invaders like Lionfish or Bullfrogs do. So Florida wildlife officials heartily encourage hunters to take as many wild hogs as they can: there are no legal protections, closed seasons or bag limits. The hogs have even become a tourist attraction of sorts, with hunters coming to Florida from all over the US to stalk the wily animals. In areas with a lot of human hunters, the Florida FWC has begun trapping pigs from other areas and relocating them where they can be shot by tourists—a win-win for everybody except the hogs. Some enterprising local restaurants and butchers have begun serving the porkers for a premium price, advertising them as "organic free-range".

But because wild pigs are fast breeders as well as being wary, adaptable and intelligent, it is probably impossible to eradicate them completely.

The Nile Monitor

In some parts of Florida, you may find yourself surprised to encounter a very large and very unfriendly dinosaur-looking lizard from Africa.

There are about 80 species of Monitor Lizard in the world, ranging across Africa and Asia and through the Indonesian Islands into Australia. They are an enormously varied group, ranging in size from small Tree Monitors only a foot long to the Komodo Dragon, the largest living lizard at around ten feet (though an extinct version in Australia was twice that size), and inhabiting everything from deserts to tropical rainforests. All are in the single genus *Varanus* (although this group's taxonomy is undergoing a lot of changes, and it is likely that a number of new species and genus may become accepted).

Unlike most lizards, which are slow, plodding, and somewhat dim-witted, the Monitors are active and inquisitive animals, quite birdlike in their actions. In lab experiments, some species have even demonstrated an ability to judge numbers and can count up to "six". Other species have been observed acting cooperatively to raid crocodile nests: one lizard lures the mother croc away, while the others then move in to dig up the eggs. In zoos, Komodo Dragons are able to distinguish individual zookeepers, and often develop bonds with their favorite humans. Because of their alert intelligence and their active diurnal lifestyles, several Monitor species have become popular in the exotic pet trade. And one of the most popular is the Nile Monitor, *Varanus niloticus*.

The Nile is a strikingly attractive lizard, with a greyish yellow throat and a glossy black body with yellow spots, stripes, and circular markings. The younger ones have the brightest colors. An adult will measure somewhere between 4 and 5 feet from nose to tail (exceptionally large ones of 7-8 feet have been recorded in the wild), and weigh around 15-20 pounds. They are noticeably more slender than most other Monitors, and their long forked tongue emphasizes their snakelike appearance. And indeed some similarities in their skull bones indicate that snakes are evolutionary descendents of a lizard group related to the Monitors — as are the ancient marine Mosasaurs. Another unique adaptation is the presence of a muscular wall between the ventricles of their heart, which makes all of the Monitors much more efficient in extracting and using oxygen to power their high-energy active lifestyle.

Because it is so tough and adaptable, the Nile is one of only five Monitor species that are not in conservation danger. The lizards range from the Nile River valley all the way down to South Africa, and although they avoid dry savannah and desert areas, they can be found along virtually every major river system.

With their bright colors, inquisitive natures, and active lifestyles, young Nile Monitors were very popular in the pet trade and were captive bred by the thousands. Sadly, though, they had a rather large drawback, of which most of the people who purchased them were unaware: unlike many of their fellow Monitor Lizards, which quickly learn to accept humans, most Nile Monitors are nervous, belligerent and defensive animals which can capably defend themselves with teeth, claws, and a long whiplike tail, and they never really become tame. A bite from even a young Nile Monitor is painful; a tail lash from a large adult can break bones. It is a lizard not to be trifled with. And so, after being bitten a couple times, many would-be keepers decided that discretion would be the better part of valor, and turned their now-unwanted pet loose.

In most areas, the released lizards were unable to survive the winters. But the Nile Monitor is adapted for a life in warm water: they spend nearly all their time along tropical African rivers, either sunning themselves on the banks, hunting for fish or small mammals, or raiding crocodile nests for eggs and hatchlings. They found

Florida, with its subtropical climate and its vast network of rivers and canals, perfectly suitable. Females dug nests in the sandbanks with up to three dozen eggs at a time. By 1990, wild populations were observed in the area around Cape Coral, and they spread quickly from there. Today they can be found from the Florida Keys up to Ft Meyers.

For the most part, Monitors will run from humans, usually by dropping into the water and swimming away. If cornered or caught, they are vicious in self-defense and can cause some damage. But their real danger is to Florida's native wildlife. It didn't take them long to take up their old nest-raiding ways, and in some areas Nile Monitors are significant predators on the nests and hatchlings of both American Alligators and endangered American Crocodiles (adult crocodilians probably return the favor by eating the adult Monitors). But the big lizards are opportunists and will also eat ground-nesting birds, rodents and other small mammals, frogs, fish, crabs, and stray cats. (On the plus side, though, they also raid and destroy Burmese Python nests.)

Fortunately, the lizards seem to have become limited in their range by the weather, and have not penetrated very far up the peninsula. In some local areas, extensive programs of trapping have eliminated them. But in other areas, they seem to be thriving.

The Africanized Honeybee

One of Florida's most famous invaders is actually a hybridized version of an earlier immigrant, one that has already been here for centuries.

The Italian Honeybee, *Apis mellifera*, has been in North America so long that most people don't even realize that it is not native. Since time immemorial, humans have been keeping hives of bees for their honey and for pollinating their fields. So when European colonists began moving to the New World in the 1500's, they took their European honeybees along with them (the Native Americans in Virginia called the new insects "the white man's fly").

In 1956, a geneticist in Brazil named Warwick Kerr decided to try to improve the plain ole ordinary Italian Honeybee by crossbreeding it with the African Honeybee of the subspecies *Apis mellifera scutellata*. The African bee lived in an environment that was much sparser than the Europeans, and consequently it had to work much harder to store sufficient food reserves for the winter. By crossing the African subspecies with the European, Kerr hoped he could develop a breed of honeybee that inherited the African genes for industriousness, resulting in a higher-producing honeybee. He imported 63 queen bees from South Africa and crossed them with Italian honeybee males from Brazil.

Unfortunately, things did not work out as planned. The African subspecies had another inborn trait: since they had to work so hard to store their winter reserves, they were also extremely aggressive in defending it, and were easily provoked into making massive stinging attacks on animals that tried to raid their supply. And, alas, the hybridized bees produced by Kerr also inherited this African trait. The hybrid Africanized bees were so aggressive in the defense of their hive that they were soon dubbed "Killer Bees".

Then a disaster happened. Kerr had been breeding his hybrid bees in a special secure lab near Rio Claro. By October 1957, he had 26 active hives, and was using a "queen excluder", a device that fit over the entrance and allowed the smaller worker bees to squeeze in and out but prevented larger queen bees from entering or exiting, to keep the hybrids in the hive and prevent them from escaping the lab. But someone mistakenly removed all the excluders, and all 26 hybridized queens headed for the open jungle, taking their African genes with them. The hybrids happily swam in the local gene pool, and soon most of the bees in the area were hybridized and had inherited the African propensity for aggressiveness. There were reports of farm animals being attacked and killed by angry swarms of Africanized bees, and soon human deaths also began to be reported.

The bees were helped by another African trait: like all bees, the Africans divided into two groups when the hive got too crowded, with a swarm flying off to form a new colony. The Italian bees only traveled a few miles away for their new hive. African bees, however, routinely swarm as far as 60 miles to establish their new homes. By the early 1960's, the Africanized hives had spread over much of Brazil. By 1986, they had moved up through Central America and reached Mexico. The United States made frantic efforts to try to prevent the "killer bees" from reaching the US: one plan was to place a large number of Italian honeybee hives in Panama to dilute the African genes as they passed through. But by 1990 the hybrid bees reached Texas, and were in California by 1993. They reached Florida in 2005.

There is no way to tell an Africanized bee from a regular Italian bee just by looking at it. The African bee is very slightly smaller, but not enough to notice. The venom in both species is the same: the African's sting is not any stronger than any normal honeybee, and like all honeybees it can only sting once before dying. The African's power comes from numbers. While European honeybees will defend their hives from threats, the Africans take this to an extreme, sending out thousands of defenders at the slightest disturbance, and actively pursuing intruders as far as 300 yards from the hive. While the "killer bee" image is exaggerated, Africanized honeybee hives have indeed caused a number of human deaths in the US.

The Africans have presented serious difficulties with Florida's commercial beekeepers, who are crucial in providing pollination for the state's agricultural businesses. In South America and Africa, beekeepers have been living with the aggressive bees for years now, and have developed methods of working with them safely. The problem in Florida is that most of the agricultural areas are also near residential areas where the bees can spread, and where people can inadvertently bother the hives and provoke an attack. The state has released a series of security guidelines for beekeepers, called "Best Management Practices", that use security measures and inspections to try to prevent Africanized queens from setting up wild hives in residential areas. All beekeepers in Florida are required to register their hives with the state. But the African hybrids are already here, and there is really no way to eliminate them. It is estimated that about 90% of all the wild honeybee hives in the southern half of Florida are now Africanized.

Currently, the Africanized honeybees can be found in most of the American Southwest and all of Florida, and are moving north at an average rate of two miles a year. Scattered reports have occurred as far north as Tennessee, probably from imported bees. In hot semi-tropical areas like Florida, the Africans can outcompete the European bees and replace them. But in cooler temperate climates, the European bees seem to have the advantage. So it is not clear just how far north the Africanized hybrids can go.

The Apple Snail

Many of Florida's invaders arrived here through the aquarium hobbyist trade, and that includes one of our recent arrivals — the Apple Snail.

There are probably thousands of freshwater snail species throughout the world. Most of them lead drab uneventful lives, munching on plants, and are of interest only to the handful of scientists who study mollusks. One such group are in the genus *Pomacea*, which contains around 30 species in South America. "Pomacea" means "apple" — the snails were named for their round shape and large size (some are as big as three inches in diameter). The Apple Snails all look much the same and have similar dull brownish bands of color, and it takes an expert to tell them apart.

Like nearly all snails, the Apple Snails are vegetarian, living on a diet of water plants and algae. Snails have a raspy tongue with many small teeth, called a "radula", which they use to scrape food into their mouths. The *Pomacea* also have their gills located inside a lunglike pouch. During warm weather when the dissolved oxygen levels in their pond are low, the snails use these gilled pouches to breathe air at the surface, and because of this they prefer to stay in shallow water near shore.

Only one of these species is native to Florida. The Florida Apple Snail, *Pomacea paludosa*, also found in Cuba and the Caribbean, is one of the smaller members of the genus. Found mostly in the Everglades, it is not very cold-tolerant and is limited to southern Florida, though it is occasionally seen elsewhere in the southeastern US where the water is artificially heated, such as power plants. Fossils show that the Florida Apple Snail hasn't changed much in several million years.

In the 1980s, pet dealers in the US began importing Apple Snails from South America for the aquarium trade. Hobbyists liked them because they were very efficient at scraping algae off the glass and keeping the tanks clean. Soon the drab brown snails were being bred in a variety of colors, including albino white, a pale blue, and a deep golden yellow. Because nobody was sure which species they actually were, they were usually sold under the name "Mystery Snails".

It wasn't long before dumped non-native Apple Snails began turning up in the wild. Florida officials first noticed them in 1987, in some canals near Lake Okeechobee. Within a short time they could be found in nearly every urban area in Florida, and across the US. By the 1990s they had reached Europe, the Philippines, Hawaii, and China.

There seemed to be several species involved. One, identified as the Spiketop Apple Snail, *Pomacea diffusa*, appears to have settled into the Florida ecosystem and is harmlessly slurping up algae. But another species turned out to be not so harmless. Initially identified as the Channeled Apple Snail, *P canaliculata*, this one was becoming an aggressive invader. Unlike the Spiketop and the native Florida Apple Snail, both of which preferred to graze on algal and bacterial pond scum, these larger Apple Snails targeted aquatic plants. Heavily-infested ponds soon became denuded, and the snails were spreading quickly, with eggs and young snails carried from one waterway to another by sticking to the feet of ducks and the bottoms of boats. By 2000, the invaders could be found in almost three-fourths of the state's surface waters. Genetic study re-identified the Mystery Snails as the Island Apple Snail, *P insularum* — and, to add to the confusion, this species was shortly later lumped together taxonomically with another as *P maculata*.

The invaders had a couple of ecological advantages over the native snails. The Mystery Snail, as well as being larger, is more cold-tolerant and can establish itself in areas where the native Florida Apple Snail cannot survive. The invasive Apple Snails also produce a greater number of eggs, which are deposited in masses on plant stems, where they resemble wads of bubble gum. The bright pink is a warning color—the eggs contain a mild toxin that protects them from predators.

The state of Florida has now taken steps to control the snails, and there are programs to find and destroy egg masses, bait and trap the adults, and treat ponds with chemical toxins that kill the mollusks. But the effect so far has been limited.

One Florida species, however, has welcomed the invaders. The Snail Kite is a small raptor which specializes in a diet of snails—particularly the native Florida Apple Snail. As drought and habitat loss reduced the number of snails, the bird's population declined to less than 1,000: it was listed as an endangered species. But as the population of invading Apple Snails has grown, so too have the birds which now feed on them. The Snail Kite has doubled its numbers in the past decade, thanks to the bonanza of Mystery Snails.

The Flamingo

The Pink Flamingo is, of course, the ubiquitous symbol of Florida, found on front lawns all over the state. Despite this, there are not actually any wild Flamingos in Florida. Or at least there haven't been for a long time — and now their presence raises the issue of just what is a "native" species and an "invader".

The Flamingo may be the most immediately-recognizable bird in the world. Almost as tall as a human, they have long legs, odd curved beaks, and a bright pink color. There are six species of Flamingo found across the world. Four of these are found in South America and the Caribbean, and two are found in Africa, southern Europe, and southern Asia. The group has undergone some confusing taxonomic changes in just the past few years. For decades, all of the Flamingos had been placed together in the genus *Phoenicopterus*, and it was believed they were related to the Ibis and Spoonbill—though some authorities argued that they were more closely related to Ducks. In 2014, new studies concluded that they were neither: the Flamingos were most closely related to the Grebes, which in turn were distant relatives of the Pigeons. Further, the single Flamingo genus was split into three. The new genus *Phoenicoparrus* contained the Andean Flamingo and the James Flamingo, both from South America, and the Lesser Flamingo from Africa was moved to its own genus *Phoeniconaias*. Remaining in *Phoenicopterus* were the Asian/African Greater Flamingo, the Chilean Flamingo from South America, and the American Flamingo, *Phoenicopterus ruber*, which ranges from Central America up to the Caribbean.

All of the Flamingos are long-legged waders that live together in huge flocks. They feed by hanging their head upside down, sucking mud and water into their curved beaks (often using their feet to stir up the muck and mud) and using their tongues to push it out through bristles inside their mouth called "lamellae". These filter out edibles like algae, brine shrimp, and bacteria. As these items are digested, they produce the pigment carotene, which the birds then incorporate into their feathers to produce their bright pink colors. In the wild, this serves as a visual signal for breeding: the better-fed the bird is, the more intense his color will be. In captivity, however, Flamingos do not obtain as much carotene from their food as they would in the wild, and so are typically paler and less intense than their wild cousins. Wild Flamingos prefer to feed in warm shallow ponds where most other aquatic life cannot survive, but where the brine shrimp and algae that they feed on thrive. To deal with the higher salt level in these evaporation ponds, the birds have special glands in their nose. Although Flamingos are non-migratory, the flocks often move around from one pond to another.

During the spring breeding season, each pair builds a nest in the mudflats that looks like a little volcano—cone-shaped with a depression on top where the single egg is laid. Both parents incubate the nest for about 30 days. Just before hatching, the unborn chick will begin chirping from inside the egg, and this is how the parents learn to recognize their particular chick out of the thousands in the flock. The hatchling is fed from a protein-rich "milk" secreted from the digestive tract of both parents. When the chick begins to leave the nest at about two weeks, it will join into large groups with other chicks, called a "creche", where each continues to be fed by its parents. The young birds are a dull grey color—they do not begin to turn their usual pink until they begin feeding on the algae and shrimp. They reach maturity in about 6 years. Zoo Flamingos have lived as long as 80 years.

When settlers from Europe arrived in Florida, they found scattered flocks of the big pink birds: apparently Florida was the northernmost extent of their range at the time. John James Audubon recorded seeing a wild flock in the Keys in 1832, and there is an account of Flamingos sitting on their nests in 1901. But at this time the trade in bird feathers—used for women's hats—was intense, and Florida's entire population of Flamingos was apparently wiped out. From the 1920s to the 50s, Flamingos were imported from the Caribbean for the tourists. When occasional birds were seen in the wild, it was presumed that they were just escapees from captive flocks. And some reported sightings were dismissed as likely mistaken identifications of the Roseate Spoonbill.

But then, in the 2010s, it began to appear as if maybe the wild Flamingos were returning to their ancestral Florida homes. Several birds were found in the Everglades that had been banded as youngsters in the wild in Mexico's Yucatan Peninsula. In 2013, a group of several dozen Flamingos appeared in a water treatment area near Boca Raton, which swelled to almost 150 birds the next year and then dropped to just a dozen the year after that. Occasional new sightings of wild Flamingos have occurred since then, as far north as Tampa Bay.

While some of these are undoubtedly escapees from captive flocks or refugees blown in by storms or hurricanes, some of them are clearly wild birds that have arrived here from somewhere else and have decided to stay—a possibility which has excited state wildlife officials, who have begun to study the birds to learn more about them. Legally, Florida classes the American Flamingo as "non-native", but present in the state as an "erratic". That classification may change if the bird actually becomes established here, again.

But so far there is one crucial factor that is missing: Flamingos require the presence of a large fellow flock in order to stimulate breeding (captive colonies often use mirrors), and since there are as yet no large wild flocks in Florida, there has been no indication that any of the recent introductions have been reproducing, and therefore they are incapable of establishing a permanent colony. Nevertheless, state wildlife officials are hopeful that more wild birds will migrate here and reach a breeding density, and that, after a century of absence, there is now a chance that the American Flamingo may finally be returning home to Florida.

The Green Basilisk

The Green Basilisk is a handsome-looking lizard: both the male and female are a bright apple-green color, and the male has showy head crests and sailfins on his back, making him look like a miniature dinosaur. But this Florida invader is probably most famous for a neat trick that has earned it the nickname of "Jesus Christ Lizard".

The basilisks, named after a monster from Greek mythology with poisonous breath that could also turn people to stone by looking at them, is a group of lizards related to the Iguanas, forming the family Corytophanidae. There are four species in one genus, all of them limited to the area of southern Mexico, Central America, and the northern part of South America.

The largest of these is the Green Basilisk, *Basiliscus plumifrons*, also known as the Crested Basilisk or the Plumed Basilisk. A resident of Central America, it is a large lizard, averaging about 2 feet and sometimes up to 3 feet in length (though most of this is tail). The females are bright green with blue and white markings; the males are similarly colored but are larger and have showy crests along their head and back which they can erect as a territorial display.

All of the basilisks are unusual among lizards because they are capable of running bipedally on their back legs for some distance, like a little T rex, as a way of escaping predators and also running down insect prey. Although their gait is ungainly (the legs are splayed out to the side, which gives them a wide waddling stance), they are capable of surprising speed over short distances. In fact, their speed combines with a special set of fringelike scales on their long toes to give them an unexpected ability—they can run across the surface of water for several feet without sinking. Their ability to "walk on water" has earned them the name by which they are widely known in Central America; the "Jesus Christ Lizard".

In the wild, they spend nearly all their time near water, usually perched on branches overhanging rivers and ponds, where they can bask at leisure in the sun and drop into the water if disturbed. They are excellent swimmers and can hold their breath underwater for almost half an hour.

In the trees they can find ripe fruit and flowers to eat, but they also hunt insects, bird eggs, and small animals. Their ability to run across the water surface allows them to dash out and snap up aquatic insects or frogs that are resting on rocks or driftwood offshore.

The adult males establish territories along their riverbank, which they defend from other males, and will try to mate with any adult female who enters. The females then dig nest burrows into the riverbank, where they lay up to 12-15 eggs. These hatch in about two to four months depending on the temperature. The youngsters are miniature copies of their parents and are fully capable of living on their own. Wild basilisks live about 7 years; in captivity they have lived to age 10. Throughout its range, the Green Basilisk is very common, and is not listed as threatened or endangered.

It was probably inevitable, though, that such interesting lizards would become popular in the pet trade. Throughout the 1990's, thousands of Green Basilisks and their cousins, the Brown Basilisks (*Basiliscus vittatus*) were imported into the US. By 1994, both species had become established in Florida, most likely as released/escaped pets. They can be found all over south Florida.

Because the lizards are skittish and don't like being around people, they are most often found in rural areas, along canals and around ponds. It is not really known how much of an effect they have on local native species — they likely make meals of small native frogs and lizards as well as bird eggs, but since the Basilisks are still somewhat limited in their Florida range and do not have a very dense population, it does not appear that their impact is very large. The Brown Basilisk species seems to be better suited to Florida than the Green, and is slowly increasing its range.

For now, the state of Florida isn't making much effort to eradicate either species. So it is likely the Jesus Christ Lizards will remain a part of the landscape.

The House Sparrow

The House Sparrow, also known as the English Sparrow, is a familiar bird in most places in the United States, including Florida. Most people who see it do not even realize that it is a non-native invader.

Like the European Starling, which was introduced to North America in New York City's Central Park, we can blame the Acclimatisation Societies in the US for the introduction of the House Sparrow. But not just one of them—this invader was intentionally released in dozens of separate areas.

Today, in a world which has become painfully aware of the environmental damage caused by humans, the very idea of an "Acclimatisation Society", with the goal of intentionally relocating plants and animals from Europe to all the other parts of the world, strikes us as odd and silly. But in the mid-19th century, the science of ecology had not even yet been born, people knew almost nothing about the natural world, and the political and social ideology of European supremacy held sway across the globe. It was considered a quite normal thing to want to reshape the rest of the world to make it more like Europe—including its wildlife. And so Acclimatisation Societies appeared all over the world, which raised money to import birds, plants, and other familiar features of the European landscape to the far-flung colonies. They had no idea how much environmental damage they were doing.

One country which enthusiastically embraced this movement was the United States. Acclimatisation Societies appeared from Philadelphia to San Francisco, and social reformers began importing everything from Chinese Pheasants to European Skylarks in an attempt to "improve the landscape". In New York City, one misguided literary's idea led to the introduction of the Starling, which still curses us today.

Another popular subject of the Acclimatisation movement was the House Sparrow, which also became known here as the English Sparrow. The Sparrows are a large family of birds within the group known as Passerines, or "perching birds". One of the most familiar of these was the House Sparrow, *Passer domesticus*, a small rather drab bird that was a common resident in nearly every city in England.

One reason why the American Acclimitasation Societies liked the House Sparrow so much was because it was one of the most common birds in London, which was at that time the center of the entire civilized world — so they wanted to be more like London. Another reason was the Sparrow's cheery song: it was assumed that if the birds were brought to the United States, as one Society put it, the "ennobling influence of the song of birds will be felt by the inhabitants." For the more practical-minded, the argument was offered that the birds would eat insect pests — which was considered an asset in a society that was still largely agrarian. Unfortunately for the future, this argument was based on a basic misunderstanding of the House Sparrow's biology: while the birds do indeed feed a large number of insects to their nestlings as they are growing up, adult Sparrows are seed-eaters — which is what you *don't* want in an agrarian society.

In the mid-19th century, the flood of Sparrows began. In 1850, Nicholas Pike, the Director of the Brooklyn Institute, paid for sixteen House Sparrows to be brought over from London and released in New York City's Central Park. They apparently died. So Pike tried again: in 1851 another one hundred birds were brought in and released, plus twenty-five more the following year. At the Brooklyn Institute, Pike raised a number of captive birds and then released them in 1853.

Other Societies followed the example. House Sparrows were imported and released in Maine, Massachusetts, Connecticut, Rhode Island, Ohio, and Nova Scotia. A thousand Sparrows were released in Philadelphia. By 1870 they were well-established across the entire northeast, and had already spread as far as South Carolina, Iowa and Montreal.

As settlers spread west, so did the birds. House Sparrows were captured in Philadelphia and New York to be relocated to Salt Lake City and San Francisco. A group of birds was even taken to Hawaii and released in 1871. Other releases took place in China, Australia, South America, and Africa. By 1900, House Sparrows could be found in virtually every sizable city in the world. In agricultural societies that depended largely upon horses for transportation, the urban birds thrived on spilled grain, street trash, and undigested seeds in the copious horse droppings.

Also by this time, however, ornithologists began to realize the devastating effect that this widespread introduction was having on native bird species. The Sparrows turned out to be prolific breeders; with 3-4 clutches per season, a single breeding pair was easily capable of raising 20 offspring each year. Not only could the invaders push out the native species through sheer numbers, but the House Sparrow also tended to nest much earlier in the year than other species—often before the migratory birds even returned for the spring—and were therefore able to occupy a majority of the best nesting sites, locking out the native birds. In many cities, the House Sparrow joined the Pigeon as the only conspicuous city-dwelling bird.

By 1910, the public's attitude towards the House Sparrow had changed: where before the aim had been to spread the species as much as possible, now the goal turned to eradication. Traps and poisons were marketed, bounties were offered for dead birds. The *Farmer's Bulletin* published a circular titled "How to Destroy House Sparrows", which declared, "the bad qualities of the bird far outweigh its good ones, and, although its extermination is impracticable, a reduction of its numbers is feasible and important. The present bulletin aims to describe the best methods of destruction."

But it was already too late. By 1930 there were an estimated 150 million House Sparrows in the US. As the automobile replaced the horse and as industrial factories replaced farms, the birds lost much of their food sources, but soon adapted: although the House Sparrow does not build up any fat reserves for the winter and is utterly dependent upon sufficient food resources to survive the cold weather, it found this in abundance as the new environmental movement enticed more and more city people to put out bird feeders. For the invaders, it was an endless supply of free food.

Now that the House Sparrow has become so widespread and ubiquitous, any efforts to control it are useless. As one state wildlife commission has noted, "Since they have already spread to most of the continent, and since their hardiness, adaptability and fecundity make them difficult to eradicate … it seems unlikely that this species can be reduced or controlled on a large scale without using aggressive (and presumably risky) methods." For the most part, efforts at controlling the Sparrow populations have only taken place in specific localities where there is a good chance of reintroducing threatened native birds like Bluebirds or Purple Martins. In the rest of the country, the House Sparrow will simply be allowed to run rampant.

The Water Lettuce

As an invader, Water Lettuce is older than the United States itself — it was first recorded in Florida way back in 1765. And now this tough little aquatic plant has become a full-fledged environmental pest.

The Water Lettuce, *Pistia stratiotes*, is the only member of its genus. It is a part of the Arum family, known scientifically as Araceae. Most of this family is aquatic, growing along lake shores.

In appearance, as the name suggests, Water Lettuce resembles a little head of partially-opened lettuce or cabbage, with thick fuzzy grooved leaves. The species was first described in the 1700's from specimens found in Africa, in the Nile River near Lake Victoria. (The name *Pistia stratiotes* means "water soldier", indicating that its aggressive qualities were known even then.) But the Water Lettuce's efficient methods of reproduction have allowed it to spread into virtually every tropical and semi-tropical area worldwide, and today no one is sure where it originally came from.

The earliest encounter in Florida came in 1765, when the explorers John and William Bartram drew and described specimens that they found in the St Johns River. Their depiction of the plant is still familiar to us today: "[We found] prodigious quantities of the *Pistia*, which grows in great plenty most of the way, and is continually driving down with the current, and great quantities lodged all along the extensive shores of this great river and its islands, where it is entangled ... all matted together in such a manner as to stop up the mouth of a large creek, so that a boat can hardly be pushed through them, though in 4 foot water."

Some fossils from the Pleistocene period indicate that members of the Water Lettuce genus may have been in Florida as long as 12,000 years ago, but some ecologists have argued that these are a different species and that our current plant is a recent arrival here, having been carried around the world in the ballast water of 17th century explorer ships. The origin of the plant has been attributed to both Africa and South America. We may never be able to tell. It is currently a pest throughout the entire southeastern US, and can be found sporadically as far north as New Jersey and as far west as Texas and California.

Like so many other Florida aquatic weeds, the Water Lettuce is free-floating, drifting about on the surface with its rootlets hanging down into the water. Although Water Lettuce can reproduce through seeds formed from inconspicuous little flowers, much of its propagation happens asexually through stolon runners that bud off little daughter plants, and these interconnected networks form dense mats which cover the water surface. A patch of Water Lettuce, under good conditions, can double its size every three weeks. The thick heavy mats can completely cover a body of water, shading it out, reducing its oxygen levels, and filling it with decomposing plant debris. Much of southern Florida has become infested with it, and many ponds, canals and slow-moving rivers have become clogged with the plant. About the only native animals which seem to appreciate the mats of vegetation are the mosquitoes, who breed among the roots, and the freshwater turtles, who eat the thick fleshy leaves.

State environmental officials have active programs to control Water Lettuce. The most common method is to use machines to either suck in the floating plants and chop them into pieces, or to rake them up onto shore where they dry out and die. There have been attempts to introduce certain insects as biological controls, but so far this hasn't been successful.

The Air Potato

The Air Potato is an odd invader from Africa. It has no flowers or seeds, but reproduces by potato-like tubers that grow on the vines – and all the new plants are clones of the parent.

The Yam family, Dioscoreaceae, has 870 different species that grow in tropical areas all around the world. Since ancient times, many species have been cultivated by humans for their large edible underground tubers, which are known by a variety of different names: manioc, yams, sweet potatoes. In many species, the rootstock contains toxins which must be leached or cooked out for the plant to be safe for humans. In the Amazon Basin and on the Pacific Islands, yams are a staple food source. Yams became particularly useful for long ocean voyages, since the underground tubers could be stored for long periods of time.

Because the yam vines have large attractive shiny leaves, some species, though inedible, have also been widely grown by gardeners as an ornamental garden plant. And one of these is *Dioscorea bulbifera*, known as the Air Potato.

The Air Potato is a stout vine with large attractive heart-shaped leaves, which have an unusual fanlike vein pattern. The name comes from the odd aerial tubers that develop at the leaf junctures: these look somewhat like a small potato, ranging from marble-sized to tennis-ball size. They are known technically as "bulbils". The thick vine climbs from the ground over trees and shrubs, often covering them completely and shading out the host, eventually killing it. The vine can grow as much as 70 feet to the very top of a tree. The underground tubers can be as much as ten inches long and weigh over ten pounds.

In the US, the vine usually dies completely back to the ground each winter, growing again from the underground tubers to full length in the spring. It is enormously fast-growing, easily reaching eight inches a day. As the vine dies in winter, the aerial bulbils drop to the ground; they are also easily rolled along by flowing water and deposited elsewhere. Each "air potato" is capable of growing a new vine. In the environmental conditions found in the US, the plants are not usually able to make their small inconspicuous white flowers or set seed, so virtually all of the propagation is done through these aerial tubers, and each new vine is a genetic clone of the one it came from.

It is not known exactly how the plant was first introduced to the United States. The most likely scenario is that it came in the late 18th century along with the African slave trade. There is some question about the edibility of *Dioscorea bulbifera:* some sources regard it as inedible, others claim that the underground tubers can be eaten after a complicated process of leaching and roasting has removed the toxins. The plant may have originally been imported as a potential food source for African slaves. The first recorded description of the Air Potato in the US was in 1777, in a garden in Mobile, Alabama.

The first definitively-known introduction in Florida came in 1905, when a few specimens were obtained by horticulturalist Henry Nehrling, who was active in the plant nursery trade near Orlando and probably sold them as ornamentals. Nehring also sent a few plants to the US Department of Agriculture and asked them to evaluate the Air Potato's usefulness as a commercial food crop. The USDA concluded that it wasn't edible, and also noted that the plant's rapid growth and ease of propagation made it a potentially dangerous invasive. But they did not ask Nehring to destroy his plants or stop selling them.

By 1993, the Air Potato had escaped numerous Florida gardens and invaded the wild, where, without any natural enemies and with perfect environmental conditions, it quickly overgrew the native trees and shrubs, shaded them out, and killed them. The invasive yams were found in 23 Florida counties, as well as parts of Alabama, Georgia, and Mississippi. By 2006 the vine infested an estimated 25% of Florida. In 1993 it was listed as a prohibited plant.

Efforts to control the Air Potato have been hampered by its biology. The buried rootstocks are invulnerable to pesticides, and the huge number of aerial tubers produced by each vine are impossible to remove once they get into the soil—even the smallest of them are able to produce a brand new vine. Even Air Potatoes that have been two-thirds eaten by squirrels or rodents can still successfully sprout.

In cooperation with the Nature Conservancy, the state began organizing local "Air Potato Roundups", in which groups of citizens would volunteer to dig up and destroy the vines and their rootstocks in local areas. These roundups removed as much as 13 tons of Air Potato plants at a time. But they were nowhere near enough to halt the plant.

In desperation, Florida officials turned to biological warfare. Once the Florida Air Potatoes were identified genetically as Chinese varieties of an African strain, the search began for some sort of biological control from its native area that would attack the vines without touching any of Florida's native vegetation. After years of research and testing, a suitable candidate was found: the Air Potato Leaf Beetle (*Lilioceris cheni*). These are small Chinese beetles that look like red or brown Ladybugs without the black spots. Both the adult beetles and the larvae feed exclusively on the leaves of the Air Potato vine. After several years of testing in special quarantine zones to confirm that the beetles did not attack any native Florida species (including our own native yam species), the first large-scale releases of the beetles were done in the Miami-Dade area in 2011. Since then, over 145,000 beetles have been released in 32 counties.

Have the beetles helped? It's too soon yet to tell. Several localities where the beetles have been released have shown a decreased amount of Air Potato and an increased amount of native vegetation, but it is not known yet if the beetles will be able to spread effectively on their own and reach wide areas of the state.

The Mediterranean Gecko

The Mediterranean Gecko hitchhiked its way to Florida and is now a familiar sight, scampering across walls and ceilings at night in its search for insects. Ironically, the Mediterranean Gecko is now in the process of being itself driven out and replaced, by a new species of fresh invader.

The Geckoes are a widespread and varied group of lizards. With over 1500 species in 7 different families, they are one of the most successful reptile groups in the world.

One of these species is the Mediterranean Gecko, also sometimes called the Turkish Gecko, *Hemidactylus turcicus*. This is a rather small lizard, about five inches long, with a flattened body and a triangular head with bulging catlike eyes. It is usually a tannish-brown color with dark rings on the tail, but depending on the temperature it can darken itself to brownish or lighten itself to almost white. The toes end in large round pads which are covered with ridges of tiny hairlike projections: with these the lizard is able to grip onto vertical surfaces and can easily climb up tree trunks, walls, mirrors, and even upside-down across ceilings.

As the name implies, the Mediterranean Gecko is found in southern Europe and northern Africa, across the Arabian Peninsula to Pakistan. It seems to have a preference for human habitations, although the Gecko is nocturnal and spends its nights running along the walls hunting for small insects. They often stake out a hunting area near artificial lights and ambush the bugs that are attracted there, then sleep during the day by pressing their flattened body inside a convenient crack or fissure. Most people probably don't even know that they share a house with them.

But although the Mediterranean Gecko seems harmless enough, it is actually one of the most successful reptilian invaders known, and is now one of the most widely-introduced lizards in the world. Small, inconspicuous and well-hidden, they make good stowaways in cargo that is carried by truck, ship, or plane. The species has now established colonies in areas far from its native home—as far as South America, southern Africa, and Asia.

In Florida, the first reports of Mediterranean Geckos came in 1915 in Key West. Apparently a stowaway on a cargo ship, this group does not seem to have established itself. But in the 1970s new appearances took place in Tampa and Miami. In the 80s and 90s the cute little lizards were popular in the pet trade, and escaped/released pets began showing up all over Florida, and soon also in Georgia, South Carolina, Louisiana, Alabama, Mississippi, Texas, New Mexico, Arizona, California, Nevada, Arkansas, Missouri, and Oklahoma. In all of these areas, the little lizards were confined to urban areas, most often living in buildings that had external lights which allowed them to easily catch prey at night.

In most of these states, there are no native Gecko species, so the ecological harm done by the invaders was minimal. But in Florida, they were able to outbreed the native Ashy Geckos, often producing two or three pairs of eggs throughout the summer. The Mediterranean Gecko's nocturnal habits also gave it an advantage: there are no native nocturnal lizards in Florida. This meant that the invaders had an entire empty ecological niche all to themselves, and their nocturnal habits made them better suited for living in human-inhabited areas than the diurnal Ashy Gecko. By the 1990's, Ashy Geckos were rare and the Mediterranean species had virtually taken over all of south Florida.

But then, competitors arrived.

The Tropical House Gecko, *Hemidactylus mabouia*, is a closely-related relative from central Africa which began appearing in Florida in the 1990s. It was quickly followed by another relative, the Indo-Pacific Gecko, *Hemidactylus garnotii*, native to Asia (also an invader in Hawaii). The two newcomers were of a similar size and had similar lifestyles, but they both had one advantage over the Mediterranean species: unlike *Hemidactylus turcicus*, which only breeds in the summer, the two new invaders could breed year-round. It didn't take long for sheer numbers to win out, and by the 2010s the Mediterranean Gecko was beginning to decline drastically in South Florida and has been largely replaced there by the Tropical House Gecko and the Indo-Pacific Gecko. But these two tropical species seem to be unable to expand their range further north, and so central and northern Florida are still the domain of the Mediterranean Gecko. Further, since it seems unlikely that the Tropical House Gecko and the Indo-Pacific Gecko can both co-exist in the same ecological niche in the south, it is likely that one will eventually out-compete the other and drive it out. Meanwhile, the native Ashy Gecko seems to be making something of a comeback, and may be able to assert itself against the two new invaders. It is anyone's guess how this situation will play itself out.

The Green Mussel

It looks like an ordinary clam. But the Green Mussel is considered by many to be one of the most stubborn and damaging of Florida's aquatic invaders.

The Green Mussel, *Perna viridis*, is a native of the warm waters of the Indian Ocean and the western Pacific, ranging from India around southeast Asia and up to China. One of the larger members of the mussel family, the Green Mussel can reach a length of over six inches. It is readily recognized by its bright green shell, which fades with age to a dull brownish with green edges.

Like all of the clams, oysters and mussels, *Perna viridis* begins life as a tiny free-floating larva, formed when male and female mussels eject clouds of sperm and eggs into the water twice a year. After a few weeks of drifting around as part of the plankton on the ocean's surface, the larva settles to the bottom in shallow water, attaches itself to a rock or piling with a series of strong fibers called byssal threads, and assumes its adult form. It will spend the rest of its life as a filter-feeder, straining edible organic particles out of the surrounding sea water.

In its native Asia, the Green Mussel is a harmless and placid resident, prized by people as seafood. As with all invasives, the problem arises when it is introduced to a non-native area where it has no natural predators. Because the large shellfish are a good food source, they have been deliberately introduced to many Pacific islands where they have escaped cultivation and become established in the wild. But most of their spread has been unintentional. Not only are the larvae easily moved around in seawater that has been pumped into the ballast tanks of ocean-going freighters, but the adult mussels readily attach themselves to ship hulls, where they are transported from place to place.

By the 1980s the Green Mussel had become established in Japan and Australia, and its potential as an invasive was demonstrated. With no natural checks on their population, the mussels quickly spread to form a solid unbroken carpet on shallow seashores, crowding out native shellfish. They covered navigation buoys (sometimes sinking them with the extra weight), clogged the pipes for power stations and water treatment plants, and choked off the flow in stormwater drains. In some areas the mussels became so thick that they lowered the oxygen content of the water, posing a threat to local fish.

During the 1980s, trade between Asia and North America grew rapidly, and as freight ships began making the trip from Japan and China to the US, the mussels hitchhiked along. By 1990 the Green Mussel had reached Venezuela, Jamaica, and Trinidad, after apparently being carried through the Panama Canal.

Just a few years later, they were in Florida. In 1999 a colony of *Perna viridis* was found clustered on an abandoned crab trap in Tampa Bay, and genetic analysis showed that they probably came from the introduced population in Trinidad. By 2003 the shellfish had spread south along the coast to Naples and had also been found, apparently independently, in the Atlantic coast cities of Jacksonville and St Augustine. A year later they were in Savannah GA and Charleston SC.

The potential impact is worrying, and state officials are closely monitoring the spread of the invaders. Already in parts of Tampa Bay the native oyster and mussel beds, which are important economically as well as ecologically, have been replaced by stands of Green Mussels. Of particular concern is the possibility that the Mussels may take over the area's extensive mangrove shores, which are vital for many native fish and marine invertebrates.

There seems to be no good way to control the Mussels. Blue Crabs and Sheepshead fish eat them, but the rate of growth is far above what the local predators can control. Although *Perna viridis* is edible by humans, it is also very efficient at concentrating pollutants from the water, which makes it potentially toxic. So although the state of Florida allows people to collect the shellfish for food, it also warns of the possible danger. For now, the Florida FWC can only hope to slow the spread of the Green Mussel by advising people to store their boats out of the water, and to carefully inspect and clean them when moving from one bay to another to help avoid carrying them around.

The good news, at least, is that the tropical Mussel cannot survive in cool waters, and its spread will likely be limited as it goes further north.

The Armadillo

The prehistoric-looking Armadillo is such a familiar part of the Florida landscape (most often as squashed roadkill along the highways) that it has become accepted as a normal part of the scenery. In reality, it is an invader in Florida, but one of the very few that got here on its own as a natural extension of its normal range.

The Armadillos are a group of about 20 mammals in the family Dasypodidae, an ancient group related to the sloths and anteaters dating back to the time just after the dinosaurs, which is characterized by a turtle-like leathery shell studded with small bone platelets that form a protective armor. At this time, sea levels were higher than they are now, so most of what is now Panama was underwater, and North and South America were separated from each other and went their separate evolutionary ways. Then about 3 million years ago, ocean levels dropped and tectonic forces pushed the land up to form the Isthmus of Panama, connecting the two continents. The result was what paleontologists refer to as the Great American Interchange, when wildlife from each continent now had a land route to the other. Deer, horses, camels, tapirs, bears and cats went south, while sloths, armadillos, giant birds and giant rodents went north.

During the Ice Ages, Florida and the rest of the southern US was inhabited by huge versions of Armadillos known as Glyptodonts, which reached the size of a Volkswagen and weighed two tons. About 10,000 years ago, however, the giant armadillos in North America died out, and only a handful of their former glory remained, in the lower half of South America.

One of these South American survivors is the Nine-Banded Armadillo, *Dasypus novemcinctus*. Measuring about two feet from nose to tail and weighing about 15 pounds, this species is marked by the nine narrow flexible bands of skin across its back which act as a hinge and allow the animal to curl up its bony outer shell for protection. The Nine-Banded Armadillo proved to be more adaptable than its fellow species, and over the years it invaded nearly all of South America, where it adapted to habitats ranging from rainforest jungle to open grassland (only the snowy peaks of the Andes Mountains were too much for it).

When the Spanish invaded South America in the 1500's, they encountered these odd-looking animals and were baffled—they had never seen anything like it before. The Aztecs had called them "turtle rabbits": the Spanish took to calling them *armadillos* ("little armored ones").

Like all the other armadillo species, the Nine-Banded Armadillo is mostly crepuscular, sleeping up to 16 hours a day and hunting at dusk and dawn, using its keen sense of smell to locate and dig up worms, insects and other soil-dwelling prey. The legs are very strong and the claws are very stout, and the Armadillo is an excellent digger, excavating subterranean chambers as shelters. Mating occurs in the summer, when the ovulating female releases one egg cell into the uterus. Once fertilized, the egg delays implantation for a few months until the weather is suitable, then it splits into four zygotes which each develops into an embryo over the next four months, producing a litter of identical quadruplets. The youngsters are weaned after about four months and wander off on their own at about nine months old.

Despite their ungainly appearance, Armadillos can run surprisingly fast. They can cross streams and rivers by holding their breath and simply walking across the bottom, but if the river is very wide, they can gulp air and float at the surface, allowing them to swim across. In South America, their primary predators are large cats like Jaguars and Cougars, which hunt them by ambush. To escape an attack, Armadillos can jump straight up into the air from a standing start, to a height of 3-4 feet. This allows them to dodge the cat's leap, and then run away. In North America, the Armadillo's only real enemy is the automobile—where their instinctive jumping response doesn't help them very much. So dead Armadillos are a common sight along roadways all across the South. In some areas, Armadillos are eaten: it is known as "poor man's pork".

At the time of the Spanish, the natural range of the Nine-Banded Armadillo lay entirely within South America. But as tough and adaptable generalists, they were already expanding their natural range, and since they were inconspicuous and harmless, the Spanish settlers mostly left them alone. By the 18th century Armadillos had expanded through Central America into Mexico, and by around 1850 they had reached the Rio Grande and crossed into the United States in Texas. Armadillos had spread to New Mexico by 1905, and reached the Florida Panhandle by 1920 and the rest of Florida by the 1950's. From there, lacking any large predators, they spread quickly northward. By the 1960's the Armadillo was firmly established in Oklahoma and across the Gulf coast states, and by the 1980's it was found in Colorado, Kansas and South Carolina. The species is expected to eventually cover most of the United States, limited only by the cold temperatures it will encounter in northern Pennsylvania and Nebraska.

For the most part, the Armadillo has been a benign invader, although some people resent its habit of digging holes in the lawn or garden, and its tendency to get hit by cars. Although it is considered a "non-native" by the State of Florida and has no legal protections, the state has taken a hands-off attitude to the "little armored one", and is making no effort to control or remove it.

The New Guinea Flatworm

Found in Florida only as recently as 2015, the New Guinea Flatworm is a voracious predator on land snails and worms, but is also a potential health threat for humans.

In the strict biological sense, the word "worm" should refer only to the group of invertebrates known as Annelids, the familiar segmented animals which include the plain ole ordinary earthworm. But most people, including biologists, have taken to referring to any long skinny slimy legless invertebrate as a "worm".

One group of "worms that aren't really worms" are the flatworms, an extremely primitive family with a very long evolutionary history. They have very simple body structures, with a head at one end and, as the name implies, a flattened body. Internally, they lack a respiratory system and breathe by absorbing oxygen through their skins. They also have no heart or blood vessels: their internal organs—what few of them there are—simply float in the blood which fills the body cavity. The stomach is a rudimentary bag with only one opening to the outside, so food goes into the same hole that the wastes come out of.

The "flukes" and "tapeworms" are modified for a parasitic life inside a host's body, but the rest of this family live in damp environments ranging from ocean floors to forest leaf litter. Nearly all of the free-living flatworms are predators who make a living by hunting snails, slugs, and other worms.

One of these is the New Guinea Flatworm, *Platydemus manokwari*. In appearance, it looks something like a skinny flat slug that is pointed at both ends, two or three inches long and brownish black in color with a noticeable orange or yellow stripe down its back. In its natural habitat in the New Guinea rainforests, this Flatworm spends its life burrowing in leaf litter and sometimes climbing up tree trunks, preying mostly on snails and worms that it locates by scent. Since it has no teeth, the Flatworm eats its prey by perching atop it, dribbling its own stomach acids out to dissolve the flesh, then sucking up the resulting nutritious soup with its mouth.

Had the New Guinea Flatworm remained in its jungle home, it would today be largely unknown, going about its wormy business unnoticed and unremarked. But in the 1990s, authorities in Guam and Okinawa were facing an invasion by the Giant African Land Snail which threatened to destroy the important agricultural industries there. Desperate for a solution, they turned to the New Guinea Flatworm. Although the two do not share a habitat and never encounter each other in the wild, officials decided that since the Flatworm eats snails, it might be effective in controlling the GALS invasion.

It didn't work out quite that way. While the Flatworms did make meals out of the African raiders, they also happily digested the local species of worms, slugs and snails as well—including several species that were found on that particular island and nowhere else. Within a short time, the Flatworms had become a serious threat to the native mollusks. Some were driven to extinction.

Meanwhile, the Flatworms were also spreading unintentionally. When potted garden plants began to be shipped in large numbers from Indonesia, the New Guinea Flatworms hitched a ride too, buried inconspicuously in the potting soil. By 2000, the predatory worms had become established in 22 different countries around the world, and began systematically hunting down and destroying the local snail populations. Although as a tropical species the worms cannot tolerate cold winters, they have even turned up in small numbers in temperate places like France—where they happily squirm their way around inside greenhouses and hothouse gardens.

In areas with large numbers of rare snail species— including many Pacific Islands—extreme measures are being taken to prevent the Flatworms from arriving. To call attention to the potential threat, the IUCN has placed the New Guinea Flatworm on its list of the "100 Most Invasive Species".

The continental United States remained safe from the voracious predators until 2015, when they turned up in gardens in Miami and Cape Coral. This produced immediate concern from state wildlife officials, since Florida is home to a large number of snail species, many of which are found nowhere else. The Flatworms also caught the attention of state health officials, since they can serve as the carrier for a small parasitic worm that normally resides in rats—in humans, the parasites can cause lung damage or meningitis.

As in the other places it has invaded, the New Guinea Flatworm has no natural predators in Florida, and it seems likely that, once introduced, it will spread throughout the state and as far north as it can go before the cold weather stops it.

The Chinese Privet

Another landscape plant that has escaped cultivation and become invasive, the Chinese Privet reverses the normal pattern — it is extensive in the northern part of Florida but has not penetrated into the south.

There are about 50 different species of Privet in the *Ligustrum* genus, all of them found in Europe, Asia and northern Africa. These are woody shrubs that grow to about 20 feet tall, with long compound leaves and dense clusters of black or blue fruits.

In Asia they are widely grown as ornamental shrubs and as hedges, and in 1852 they were imported into the US. Gardeners here liked the plants because they were hardy, attractive, and could tolerate high levels of pollutants in the air and soil.

Most of the imported Privet species behaved themselves and became common ornamental garden shrubs, such as the Wax Privet *Ligustrum lucidum*. Some species, however, were not so well-behaved, and demonstrated a marked tendency to invade and take over uncultivated areas. And chief among these was the Chinese Privet, *Ligustrum sinense.*

Chinese Privet is an attractive plant with white flowers and bright blue fruit. It was widely planted in the southeast as an ornamental, but once it escaped cultivation it revealed its talents as an invader. In a native southeastern forest, the understory is usually open and sunny, with a variety of herbaceous plants and palmettos. The shrubby Privets are able to exploit this niche by growing more rapidly and taller than the natives, outcompeting them and forming an unbroken undercanopy which shades out everything underneath it. In effect, the invader is utilizing an ecological niche which had not previously existed in the area.

By the 1930s Chinese Privet had spread across the Carolinas and all the way down into north Florida. Privets prefer disturbed low-lying moist areas in forested habitats, especially along streams. Here they can form dense thickets which crowd out native plants, and the large amount of leaf litter which they produce can prevent the spouting of other seedling trees and ground plants. Privets are a demonstrated threat to Florida's endangered Miccosukee Gooseberry, *Ribes echinellum.*

In humans, the pollen of the Privet plant is known to cause allergies and hay-fever symptoms.

Although Privets are reported to be toxic to cattle and other livestock, the blue fruits are eaten by native Florida animals such as deer, bobwhite quail, and other birds, and this also helps to spread the plants by depositing seeds further afield. The Privet's affinity for wet low-lying areas also allows it to survive wildfires and then spread into the depopulated areas.

In Florida, the Chinese Privet is mostly limited to the northern part of the state, though there has been a population found in the Miami-Dade area. It is classed as a Category I invasive, and it is illegal to grow or possess. Although the plant is vulnerable to herbicides such as glyphosate, the cost to treat such large areas is usually prohibitive. Instead the state has focused its attention on halting the spread of Privet through hand-clearing areas where it is not yet established, by pulling out seedlings and digging out rootstocks.

In 1959, a natural predator of the Privet family, the Ligustrum Seed Weevil (*Ochyromera ligustri*) was found in North Carolina, where it had apparently been unintentionally introduced in the garden trade. Since then it has spread across the southeast. This weevil attacks the seeds and leaves of invasive Chinese Privet — but it also harms the non-invasive Japanese Privet. So far the insect has not had a noticeable effect on the spread of Privets. In New Zealand, where Privets are a serious problem, the Privet Lace Bug (*Leptoypha hospita*) has been imported as a biological control agent

The landscaping industry has now developed a sterile variety of Privet called "Sunshine", with yellowish leaves. This version was developed to be suitable as a hedge plant and garden ornamental, but to be incapable of reproducing and becoming invasive. State officials also encourage people to utilize the native Florida Swamp Privet, *Forestiera segregata*, as a landscape plant instead of the non-natives.

The Common Mynah

The Mynah bird has long been popular in the pet trade because of its intelligence, its brash personality, and its remarkable ability to mimic human speech.

The Mynahs are members of the Sturnidae family of birds, along with the Starlings. There are two distinct genera: the "true mynahs" are in the genus *Acridotheres*, and the similar "hill mynahs" are in *Gracula*. Geographically, the Mynahs range from southern Europe to Iran and across Asia through India to Java. Genetic and fossil evidence indicates that they first evolved from an African starling about 5 million years ago, as the last Ice Age began.

Taxonomically, however, this entire family is a mess, and there is much debate among ornithologists over how many species there are and which genus they belong to. It is however generally agreed that there are at least eight species in the genus *Acridotheres* (the Latin name means "grasshopper hunter"), and that one of the most widespread of these is the Common Mynah *Acridotheres tristis*, which can be found in most of southern Asia.

About the size of a Grackle, the Mynah is a rusty black color with yellow legs and a strip of white along the side of its body. The most prominent markings are a wide yellow ring around the eyes and large white patches on the wings that are visible in flight. Males and females look the same.

Ecologically, the Mynahs are generalists. Most of their time is spent on the ground hunting for food (they are unusual in that they can stride easily on two legs and do not "hop" like most birds). They will eat a variety of fruits including apples, grapes, strawberries, mangoes and guavas, and also cereal grains like corn, wheat and rice. As their genus name suggests, though, much of their diet consists of ground-dwelling insects. Mynahs prefer to live near humans and are not often found outside of cities, where they settle down in open areas like parks, cemeteries, and shopping malls. Their crop-raiding habits make them a serious pest in agricultural areas.

The birds roost together in large flocks, where they are noisy, raucous, and quarrelsome, both with each other and with other nearby birds. Like their relatives the Starlings, Mynahs are adept at learning to mimic human speech. This ability to "talk" made them tremendously popular; Mynahs were a favorite at medieval royal courts and in Victorian London society, and the birds were shipped all over the world by fanciers.

In some cases, the introduction of Mynahs was deliberate. In 1856, a group of birds was released into Hawaii in the hopes that they would eat the army-worms and cut-worms that were attacking the island's sugar plantations. A century later in 1968, a set of 100 Mynahs was introduced into Canberra, Australia, to control insects. And in other cities across the world, escapees and freed pets established their own colonies.

Tough, intelligent, and aggressive, the birds soon began to take over. Although best-suited for tropical conditions, Mynahs are adaptable and can tolerate occasional freezing conditions. During the breeding season the birds nest in cavities and other protected places, and will fiercely defend their nesting territory from other birds. They will also drive other birds from their shelters and take them over. Captives have lived up to 12 years, though wild ones probably don't last half that long.

Today, the Common Mynah has successfully established itself in cities on nearly every continent, and is listed by the International Union for the Conservation of Nature as one of the "100 Worst Invasive Species" — one of the few bird species to make that list. In Hawaii, where it was intentionally introduced, it has spread to every island and is crowding out native bird species. In Australia, Mynahs are a serious threat to native parrots and cockatoos, by driving them out of nest cavities. In South Africa, where escaped pets established themselves, they have become such pests that people are encouraged to shoot them. Invasive Mynahs can also be found in Russia, Madagascar, New Zealand, Hong Kong, Canada, Argentina, several Pacific islands, and many other places.

In Florida, the first breeding colonies appeared in Miami in 1983, apparently the result of escapees and released pets. The import of Mynah birds into the US has now been banned — but it is already too late. (And because they are so popular and so expensive, Mynahs are still being illegally smuggled into the country for bird fanciers.) The birds can be found in over 20 Florida cities, ranging all the way up into Georgia. Mynahs are a danger to Florida's native Purple Martins and Bluebirds, by driving them away from nesting sites.

Fortunately, the Mynah populations in Florida have so far not been expanding very rapidly and seem to be limited to the urban areas. Although state wildlife officials doubt that the birds can be completely eradicated, they are hopeful that they can at least be prevented from spreading.

The European Human

By far the most destructive species ever to invade Florida, it could be argued, were humans from Europe.

On March 3, 1513, Juan Ponce de Leon left the Puerto Rican port of Punta Aguada with three ships and sailed north. De Leon had traveled from Spain to the New World on Columbus's second voyage in 1493, becoming a Provincial Governor on the island of Hispaniola and then Governor of Puerto Rico. According to legend, de Leon's latest voyage was in search of the fabled island of Bimini, where the Fountain of Youth was said to be located. In reality, de Leon was searching for the same things every Spanish Conquistador searched for—land and gold.

On April 2, during the Easter Week Festival of Flowers, de Leon sighted land near the present-day St Johns River, and, thinking he had found another Caribbean island, he named it *La Florida* ("the flowered land") in honor of the holiday. He had, unknowingly, landed on the shore of an entirely new continent. (De Leon found that he was not the first European to reach Florida, though—one of the Timucua natives that he met onshore spoke a few words of Spanish, likely taught to him by a shipwrecked sailor or pirate.) After sailing for Spain and receiving a royal appointment as Governor of Florida, de Leon returned in 1521, was wounded by an arrow in a fight with the Florida natives in the vicinity of modern-day Naples, and sailed to Cuba where he died of infection.

The original inhabitants of Tampa Bay were the Tocobaga Nation, who were allied with the powerful Calusa group that covered most of southern Florida. The first European to land in Tampa Bay was Narvaez in 1528. Finding no gold, he stayed only a short time. He was followed in 1540 by Hernan De Soto. De Soto also moved on after finding no gold.

It wasn't until years later that any serious attempt was made by the Spanish to settle a colony in Florida. In

1559, Tristán de Luna y Arellano founded a small Spanish town near what is now Pensacola, but within two years the colony had been hit by hurricanes, attacked by local natives, and suffered famine brought about by crop failures, and was abandoned. By this time the French had also reached Florida, and in 1562 the French Huguenot Jean Ribault landed at the St Johns River before sailing further north and starting an unsuccessful colony called Charlesfort, on what is now Parris Island, South Carolina. In 1564, another French Huguenot who had sailed with Ribault, named René Goulaine de Laudonnière, landed at the "River of Dolphins", now the Matanzas River, and built a palisaded stronghold called Fort Caroline. The Spanish King sent Pedro Menéndez de Avilés to establish a Spanish base in the area and expel the French. Avilés landed at a nearby native Timucuan village on August 28, 1565, with about 800 troops and colonists, and obtained permission from the local chief to build a wooden fort next to the village. Since it was the Feast Day of St Augustine of Hippo, the new Spanish settlement was named St Augustine.

By the end of the 16th century, European diseases had wiped out nearly all the Tocobaga and Timucua people, then spread into the rest of Florida and killed nearly the entire native population.

Now virtually empty and considered worthless swampland, Florida was given to Britain in 1763 under the treaty ending the Seven Years War, then was given back to Spain in the Treaty of Paris in 1783 (which also granted independence to the United States). By the mid 18th century, bands of Creek natives from Georgia had moved into the largely unpopulated areas of Florida, and formed the Seminole culture. The Spanish also tried to expand their small settlements to turn Florida into a viable colony, founding Miami in 1810 with settlers from the Caribbean.

When the US purchased Florida from Spain in 1821, the US military moved in to establish forts, and conflict with the Seminoles was inevitable. In a series of three Seminole Wars, the natives were driven into the inaccessible Everglades. Florida became a State in 1845.

For the first few decades of its existence, two obstacles slowed the State's growth. One was the lack of reliable transportation—Florida has relatively few navigable rivers, and building roads through the extensive swampland was difficult and expensive. As a result, most of the state's residents lived along the coasts while the interior remained virtually empty. The other obstacle was the tropical climate, which was not only hot and uncomfortable, but produced lethal outbreaks of tropical diseases like yellow fever and malaria.

The first of these problems was overcome by two new railroads, one built along the east coast of Florida by Henry Flagler, and the other running across the peninsula to Tampa Bay, built by Henry Plant. These links connected Florida to the rest of the US, and this easy flow of people and products allowed the population to expand, fed by the tourist trade that became established along the beach areas.

The second problem was solved with an intensive campaign of spraying to eliminate the mosquitoes that carried tropical diseases. After World War II, they were virtually eradicated. In the 1950's, therefore, when air conditioning became widespread, Florida's population began to balloon. Between 1960 and 2010, Florida's population quadrupled from 5 million to 20 million, making it the fourth most populated state in the US.

The inflow of people led to massive road networks and the replacement of wild habitat by citrus groves, phosphate mines, and other economic activities, which destroyed much of the habitat and split the rest into small fragments. Wetland areas were drained, mangrove swamps were bulldozed for expensive vacation houses, and the flatlands were turned into strip malls and housing developments. The destruction of the Everglades began in 1905, when former Governor Napoleon Broward began the first large-scale projects to drain the area through a network of canals. By 1948 the US Congress funded the "Central and South Florida Project", which used the Army Corps of Engineers to dig thousands of miles of canals and levees to stop the flow of water in the Everglades, then drain it to produce agricultural land. By the 1960's only a tiny remnant of the original Everglades still remained.

The effect of all this on Florida's wildlife was devastating. Species after species, including Alligators, Manatees, Key Deer, Bald Eagles, Pelicans, and Florida Scrub Palmetto, lost their habitats and dwindled close to extinction. In the 1960's, Florida finally began to take steps to protect its natural habitats and wildlife, partly as a result of the environmental movement and partly from economic self-interest (Florida's wild areas were and still are a major component of the state's tourist economy). Areas of land were purchased and set aside as state parks and wildlife refuges, laws were passed to protect wildlife and to regulate commercial development, especially along the shores, and a massive project was undertaken to restore the natural flow of water to the Everglades.

Many of these efforts have been successful; several species have been brought back from the brink of extinction and a few have even been "de-listed" from the endangered species rolls. But as Florida's population continues to grow and as economic interests once again begin to dominate the agenda of the state's government, the challenges of environmental protection will continue to face the state into the foreseeable future.

www.ingramcontent.com/pod-product-compliance
Lightning Source LLC
Chambersburg PA
CBHW060849280326
41934CB00007B/973